QUANTITATIVE CRIMINOLOGY

Volume 24
SAGE RESEARCH PROGRESS SERIES IN CRIMINOLOGY

SAGE RESEARCH PROGRESS SERIES IN CRIMINOLOGY

Published in Cooperation with the American Society of Criminology
Series Editor: **MICHAEL R. GOTTFREDSON,** *State University of
    New York at Albany*
Founding Series Editor: **JAMES A. INCIARDI,** *University of Delaware*

SAGE RESEARCH PROGRESS SERIES IN CRIMINOLOGY
VOLUME 24

QUANTITATIVE CRIMINOLOGY
Innovations and Applications

edited by **JOHN HAGAN**

Published in cooperation with the
AMERICAN SOCIETY of CRIMINOLOGY

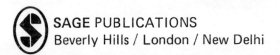

SAGE PUBLICATIONS
Beverly Hills / London / New Delhi

For information address:

SAGE Publications, Inc.
275 South Beverly Drive
Beverly Hills, California 90212

SAGE Publications India Pvt. Ltd.
C-236 Defence Colony
New Delhi 110 024, India

SAGE Publications Ltd
28 Banner Street
London EC1Y 8QE, England

Printed in the United States of America

Library of Congress Cataloging in Publication Data

Main entry under title:

Quantitative criminology.

(Sage research progress series in criminology ; v. 24)
Contents; Interrupted time series analysis of uniform
crime reports / Richard McCleary, Barbara C. Nienstedt,
James M. Erven — A further test of the stability of
punishment hypothesis / Richard A. Berk, David Rauma,
Sheldon L. Messinger — Longitudinal models, missing
data, and the estimation of victimization prevalence /
William F. Eddy, Stephen E. Fienberg, Diane L. Griffin—
[etc.]
    1. Crime and criminals—Research—United States—
Addresses, essays, lectures. 2. Criminal justice,
Administration of—Research—United States—Addresses,
essays, lectures. I. Hagan, John, 1947-
II. Series.
HV6024.5.Q36 1982   364'.973   82-20442
ISBN 0-8039-0948-9
ISBN 0-8039-0949-7 (pbk.)

FIRST PRINTING

CONTENTS

John Hagan

University of Wisconsin-Madison

INTRODUCTION
Methodological Innovation in the
Study of Crime and Punishment

Criminological research has undergone some significant changes in the past several decades. Among the most striking of these changes has been the increase in attention paid to the use of quantitative methods. If the 1960s and '70s were years of theoretical innovation in criminology—and they surely were with the rise of labelling, conflict and Marxist theories of crime, and the emergence of the Critical and New Criminologies—then the 1980s are promising to be years of methodological innovation. Proof of the latter is seen in the publication of volumes like David Greenberg's *Mathematical Criminology* (1979) and James Fox's *Methods in Quantitative Criminology* (1981a) and *Models in Quantitative Criminology* 1981b). It is also seen in the willingness—indeed, in the enthusiasm—with which many of those most interested in the newer and politically more radical theories of crime have subjected their hypotheses to quantitative tests (e.g., Greenberg, 1977; Jacobs, 1979; Lizotte, 1978).

Of course, things have not always been as we have just described. The benefits (e.g., McDonald, 1976) and liabilities (Quinney, 1969, 1973; Taylor et al., 1973; Beirne, 1979) of the use of quantitative methods in criminological research were debated heatedly in the 1970s, and the vestiges of this debate have lingered in the 1980s (see Beirne, 1980; Jacobs, 1980; Greenberg, 1980). However, it is also clear by now that quantitative criminology has made important contributions to the newer as well as older theoretical traditions.

The chapters in this volume address new and old issues in methodologically innovative ways. Each is an example of the use of quantitative techniques in a creative fashion. The *creative* potential of the application of quantitative techniques in criminological research has not always been recognized. However, quantitative criminology has increasingly become a critical context in which new ideas are matched with new kinds of data and new modes of analysis. Often this has required the charting of new methodological and unexplored theoretical domains, and it has often led to new ways of conceiving and of doing our work. The chapters described below exemplify this trend.

McCleary, Nienstedt, and Erven's study of the effects of organizational reforms on Uniform Crime Reports is a striking example of the creative potential of quantitative criminology. Taking Kitsuse and Cicourel's classic discussion of official statistics as their starting point, the authors use the techniques of interrupted time series analysis to examine the impact of the changing structures of three police departments on the crime statistics they generate. To do this, incidental or unplanned changes in these departments are treated as "natural" or "time series quasi-experiments" and analyzed using the Auto Regressive Integrated Moving Average (ARIMA) models developed by Box, Tiao, and Jenkins. The results are striking in showing the prominent role variations in organizational structure can play in determining official crime statistics.

For example, in the first department studied, McCleary et al. found evidence for the generalization that official crime rates will vary with the relative use of different kinds of investigation. In this particular case the comparison is between specific investigations conducted by detectives and general investigations conducted by patrol officers. The former are technicians and therefore more adept at applying formal definitions to cases. In City A, specific investigations were mandated for all burglary complaints. The consequence was that coding errors, and in turn the official crime rate, declined.

In the second department studied, McCleary et al. found evidence for the generalization that the official crime rate will be a function of organizational goals. To subject the crime rate to organizational goals, it is noted that hierarchical control over complaint processors is required. This control dissipated with the retirement of an incumbent police chief in the second department, and the result was an increase in UCR burglaries.

The third department illustrates the effects of a typical screening structure on the official crime rate. In this department, sergeants relied on complainant characteristics, particularly race, to screen out cases. The consequence was that in this department complaints from ghetto areas were less likely to result in dispatched service calls. This in turn had the effect of reducing the official crime rate.

The combined findings from these three departments cannot form the basis for a fully specified theory of official crime rates; nonetheless, they demonstrate the utility of using time series methods to analyze relationships between organizational structures and these rates.

Chapter 2, by Berk, Rauma, and Messinger, explores "the stability of punishment hypothesis" in a novel way. Since Durkheim, it has been argued that societies tend toward stable levels of punishment. However, as Berk et al. point out, while the work of Blumstein and several co-authors has often seemed to confirm this hypothesis, their own recent research does not (see Berk et al., 1981). To date, research testing the stability of punishment hypothesis has predicted that the proportion of people sanctioned will approximate closely a constant fraction of the society's population. In the current chapter Berk et al. instead "monetize" this hypothesis, suggesting that the expected stable ratio be conceived as the amount of money spent on punishment over the total spent on all other public expenditures. The question they then effectively try to answer is whether there might exist some balance between how much a society pays to punish its criminals and how much it pays for other public services. The time series data used to answer this question are for the state of California from 1860 to 1970.

The results reported in this particular analysis are not supportive of a monetized version of the stability of punishment hypothesis. However, Berk et al. do not rule out the possibility that other dynamic equilibrating processes may apply. They also provide some qualified evidence that "partial adjustment models" may help to explain expenditures on punishment. Thus, even if the traditional stability of punishment hypothesis cannot be confirmed, it still may be possible to explain historical variations in corrections budgets using the kinds of models explored in the latter part of this chapter.

The third contribution to this volume is by Eddy, Fienberg, and Griffin on the use of National Crime Survey (NCS) data for the estimation of victimization prevalence. These data have been used since the inception of the survey to produce incidence rates by crime type and selected victim/offender characteristics. This chapter represents an initial effort to develop stochastic models for victimization that yield annual prevalence rates. The complement to the previous measure—the percentage of crime-free households in a given year—is also considered.

The attempt to estimate prevalence makes manifest a number of features of the National Crime Survey that require careful consideration. For example, it is necessary in these surveys to distinguish between the housing unit or location, the household or family living in that unit, and the individuals who compose the household. It is also necessary to fit together in a meaningful way interviews with respondents for successive periods to provide full and comparable coverage. The problems, then, involve organizing the data by appropriate units and periods of coverage in order to make meaningful estimates of prevalence. Added to this are problems of missing data by unit and period considered.

Eddy et al. take the first crucial steps involved in addressing these problems. Several "naive" stochastic models are developed in which kinds of data we have been talking about are assumed to be missing at random. The development of these models obviously involves simplifying assumptions, and they are made for the purpose of building a comparative base for the work that is to follow. One important contribution of this initial exercise is the indication that missing data present a far greater problem for rotating panel surveys than has been acknowledged by those who have conducted these surveys in the past. It also is suggested that since "missingness" itself is quite plausibly related to victimization, attention should be paid in the future to modeling missingness and victimization simultaneously. Chapter 3 clearly charts the path of important work to come.

Although it is commonly noted that the movement of individuals through a criminal justice system is processual, Marjorie Zatz's chapter, "Dynamic Models of Criminal Processing Histories," points out that the use of processing models is nonetheless rare in criminal justice research. This chapter describes a multivariate, finite-state, continuous-time, stochastic model for the study of the criminal processing of individual defendants. An attraction of such an approach is that it allows for the development of formal models of criminal justice processing that give explicit consideration to the way potential outcomes are interrelated over time. Official histories of processing events form the data base for the research. Transitions between categorical states in the criminal justice process are the units of analysis, and the dependent variable is the unobserved instantaneous rate of transition between the states. Maximum-likelihood estimates of instantaneous rates of transition between categorical states are obtained through the use of the program "RATE." The transition rates are modeled as functions of exogenous variables.

Using a contemporary California data set, instantaneous rates of transition are modeled from the state of arrest to three disposition states (police release, prosecution denial of complaint, and lower or superior court). Models are developed for each processing of the defendant, or for what is called each "shift." Within each of these shifts, direct and interaction effects of race/ethnicity and other exogenous variables on rates of moving from arrest to case disposition are examined. Differences are reported among racial/ethnic groups across shifts to each of the three outcome states. As Zatz notes, one of the most important contributions of using this approach is to make us reconceptualize recidivism as an *aspect* of criminal justice processing rather than as a defendant status. What is being done with this approach is to focus attention on whether rates of transition differ for initial or later processings of the *same* individuals. This approach represents a promising innovation in the study of disparities in criminal justice processing.

Michael Hout's chapter explores the use of the uniform association model with survey data on delinquency. His concern is that when there is information about the ordering of cross-classified data, it is inefficient to use the general log-linear model. The name given to the uniform association model derives from the implication it carries that differences among the elements of "the basic set of interactions" are not statistically significant; in other words, the implication is that these elements are "uniform."

The data for this application of the uniform association model are taken from Gary Jensen's (1972) test of the differential association perspective. Data from a 3x3x3 cross-classification of self-reported delinquent acts, number of delinquent friends, and attitudes toward breaking the law form the basis of the analysis. The parameter estimates reported are obtained from a program developed by Haberman called FREQ. Substantively, the analysis shows that not only are the self-reported delinquent acts of the white youths studied related to the number of delinquent friends they associate with and the favorableness of their attitudes toward breaking the law, but also that these relationships are uniform. Thus the odds of delinquency increase log-linearly with each increase in delinquent friendships and pro-delinquent attitudes. Hout notes in closing that the uniform association model is powerful in the sense that it fits a single parameter (one degree of freedom) to each two-way association. If an association is linear and additive with categories that are equally spaced, the uniform association model can detect a small but significant association that might be missed by the general log-linear model.

The chapter by Alan Lizotte, James Mercy, and Eric Monkkonen exemplifies the trend noted at the outset of this discussion toward quantitative tests of hypotheses derived from the newer and more radical theories. The structural form of these theories often has required the development of new types of measures appropriate to the kinds of concepts considered. In Lizotte et al.'s analysis of crime and police strength in Chicago from 1947 to 1970, the emphasis is on developing a new measure of inequity of power. The argument presented is that Marx's notion of the rate of surplus value is the proper way to conceptualize power inequity. The operationalization of the rate of surplus value applied here consists of the value of shipments in manufacturing, less wages to production workers and costs of materials, all divided by the wages of production workers.

Intriguing results follow from the inclusion of this measure of the rate of surplus value in models attempting to explain police strength. Most significantly, perhaps, the analysis suggests that the rate of surplus value in manufacturing, along with other indicators of the strength of capital, explain all of the effect of black population size on either police strength or crime. The implication of this finding, as Lizotte et al. note in their conclusion, is that "the police are not powerful for racism's sake, but for capital's sake." The authors also offer some interesting extensions of their ideas to explain patterns of crime found in earlier eras by Shaw and McKay. These findings should serve to enliven the new and growing literature on crime and police strength.

This introduction has attempted to make clear that the chapters to follow do not speak merely to issues of method, although they clearly and creatively do that. My point is that they collectively also contribute to the development of criminological theory. Ideas as far apart as those of Marx, Durkheim, Shaw and McKay, Sutherland, Chambliss and Seidman, and Kitsuse and Cicourel have been explored in these pages. It is in this spirit of theoretical exploration and elaboration that the methodological innovations of the 1980s promise to make some of their most important contributions to modern criminology.

REFERENCES

BEIRNE, P. (1980) "Some more on empiricism in the study of law: a reply to Jacobs." Social Problems 27: 471-75.
——— (1979) "Empiricism and the critique of Marxism on law and crime."
BERK, R. A., D. RAUMA, S. L. MESSINGER, and T. F. COOLEY (1981) "A test of the stability of punishment hypothesis: the case of California, 1851-1970." Amer. Soc. Rev. 46: 805-828.
FOX, J. (1981a) Methods in Quantitative Criminology. New York: Academic Press.
——— (1981b) Models in Quantitative Criminology. New York: Academic Press.
GREENBERG, D. (1980) "A critique of the immaculate conception: a comment on Beirne." Social Problems 27: 476-477.
——— (1979) Mathematical Criminology. New Brunswick, NJ: Rutgers Univ. Press.
——— (1977) "Delinquency and the age structure of society." Contemporary Crises 1: 189-224.
JACOBS, D. (1980) "Marxism and the critique of empiricism: a comment on Beirne." 27: Social Problems 467-470.
——— (1979) "Inequality and police strength: conflict theory and coercive control in metropolitan areas." Amer. Soc. Rev. 44: 913-925.
JENSEN, G. (1972) "Parents, peers and delinquent action: a test of the differential association perspective." Amer. J. of Sociology 78: 562-575.
LIZOTTE, A. (1978) "Extra-legal factors in Chicago's criminal courts: testing the conflict model of criminal justice." Social Problems 25: 564-580.
McDONALD, L. (1976) The Sociology of Law and Order. Boulder, CO: Westview Press.
QUINNEY, R. (1973) Critique of the Legal Order. Boston: Little, Brown.
——— (1969) The Social Reality of Crime. Boston: Little, Brown.
TAYLOR, I., P. WALTON, and J. YOUNG (1973) The New Criminology. London: Routledge & Kegan Paul.

2

Richard McCleary
Barbara C. Nienstedt
James M. Erven
Arizona State University

INTERRUPTED TIME SERIES ANALYSIS
OF *UNIFORM CRIME REPORTS*
The Case of Organizational Reforms

The oldest, most comprehensive source of crime statistics is the Uniform Crime Reports (UCR), published annually by the FBI. Although more widely used than other crime statistics, the UCR is not necessarily more valid or reliable than alternative statistics. It ignores crimes that fall outside the eight "index" categories, for example, as well as crimes not reported to local police departments (Hindelang, 1976; Skogan, 1974, 1976). Government agencies nonetheless rely heavily on UCR for monitoring crime control programs, and when politicians complain that crime rates are up or brag that crime rates are down, they invariably mean that UCR crime rates are up or down. UCR in this most important sense, then, reports the official crime statistics for most U.S. cities and states.

Organizational structures which may threaten the validity of UCR is our major concern in this essay. This problem has been addressed to some extent as the "production of crime rates" (Black, 1970; Maxfield et al., 1980), but the most general statement of this problem is the classic "Note on the Use of Official Statistics" by Kitsuse and Cicourel (1963: 137):

> [Crime] rates can be viewed as indices of organizational processes rather than as indices of the incidence of certain forms of behavior. For example, variations in the rates of deviant behavior among a

AUTHORS' NOTE: Order of authorship is intended. A version of this chapter was presented at the annual meeting of the American Society of Criminology, Washington, D.C., November 1981.

given group (e.g., Negroes) as reflected in the statistics of different organizations may be a product of the differing definitions of deviant behavior used by those organizations, differences in the processing of deviant behavior, differences in the ideological, political, and other organizational conditions which affect the rate-making process.

Two jurisdictions may thus have different UCR rates because of differences in real crime or, as Kitsuse and Cicourel suggest, because of differences in the way the jurisdictions process complaints.

Organizational theorists view the organization as a "black box" with observable inputs and outputs. Different input-output chains are attributed to differences in black box structures. Research from this perspective traditionally relies on correlational designs and controlled experiments. Organizations which differ on some known structural dimension, for example, permit a cross-sectional examination of the relationship between structure and input-output chains. Alternatively, in single organizations, structures may be manipulated experimentally to reveal that relationship.

By analogy with organizational theory, "real" crime is an input to the police department and UCR is an output. But since "real" crime inputs are seldom known, the structural correlates of crime-UCR chains are not easily analyzed with cross-sectional designs. And because researchers cannot ordinarily manipulate the organizational structure of a police department, classical experiments must also be ruled out.

The structures of police departments do change over time, however, though seldom experimentally and usually not by conscious plan. These incidental or unplanned changes constitute a class of "natural experiments" (Campbell, 1969) which may be analyzed to reveal the relationship between structural variables and the crime-UCR chain. A research design often used to study "natural experiments" is the time series quasi-experiment which, using the conventional notation of Campbell and Stanley (1966), may be diagrammed as

$$0 \quad 0 \quad 0 \quad 0(X)0 \quad 0 \quad 0 \quad 0$$

Each 0 represents an observation of a process and the X represents an intervention. Together the observations are a time series, divided into pre- and postintervention segments by the intervention. The most widely used statistical models for analysis of the time series quasi-experiment are the Auto Regressive Integrated Moving Average (ARIMA) models of Box and Tiao (1965, 1975; Box and Jenkins, 1976). In this essay, we demonstrate the use of ARIMA time series models to analyze three UCR time series. In each of our three examples, unplanned organizational changes are hypoth-esized to have an impact on official crime rates. After describing the results of these three quasi-experiments, we develop a minimal theory of crime rates as organizational outcomes.

CASE 1:
INVESTIGATION AS A MEDIATING VARIABLE

Figure 1 shows monthly UCR burglaries in a major southwestern city (identified only as "City A") from January 1975 to May 1981. Burglary complaints in City A are not normally investigated beyond the simple field reports filed by uniformed officers as part of the routine, formal com-plaint procedure. For a 21-month period, however, all burglary complaints in City A were formally investigated by detectives. The level of the UCR burglary series drops abruptly with onset of this program and then rises abruptly with its termination. We conclude from this evidence that the program effectively reduced UCR burglaries in City A, but, of course, the causal mechanism for this reduction is unknown.

The two most obvious explanations for the reduction can be ruled out immediately. First, the program was expected to increase the rate of burglary "clearances." Had this goal been realized, one might expect an eventual reduction in burglaries, but not the immediate reduction shown in Figure 1. A second, more cynical explanation—that the detectives reduced UCR burglaries by "cheating"—may also be ruled out. If this effect were due to a simple conspiracy, one would expect a coincidental effect on burglary clearances. Since clearances did not increase during this period, we can rule out both of these explanations.

A less obvious explanation is that the experimental program somehow changed the procedures by which burglary complaints become UCR burglaries. The three events which constitute complaint-processing are an official complaint taken from the victim by uniformed officers, an inves-tigation by detectives, and a coding decision by UCR coding clerks. Under normal circumstances (that is, before and after the experimental program), uniformed officers are dispatched to the scene of a burglary to take a formal complaint from the victim. The uniformed officers conduct a pro forma investigation at that time, securing descriptions of stolen property, checking for physical evidence, and so forth. If the site investigation produces no investigative leads, however, which is ordinarily the case, there is no follow-up investigation by detectives.

The next event in the complaint-processing flow is a UCR coding decision. Coding decisions are made directly from the field reports filed by the uniformed officers at the scene. Our interviews with UCR coding

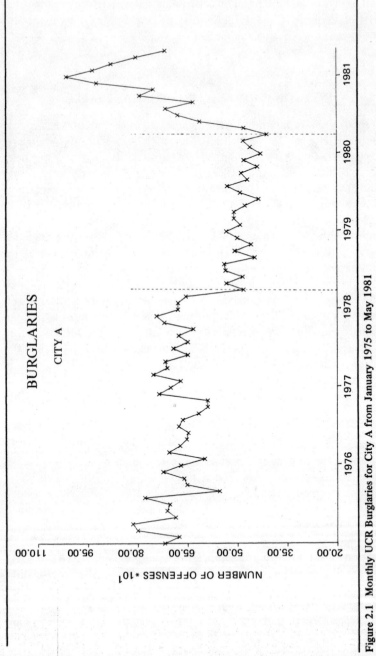

Figure 2.1 Monthly UCR Burglaries for City A from January 1975 to May 1981

NOTE: Vertical dotted lines indicate onset and termination of an experimental program.

clerks suggest that it was this aspect of complaint-processing that changed during the experimental program.[1] As it turns out, the field reports are unreliable, with errors falling into three common categories.

(1) *Definitional misunderstandings:* Many complaint report errors are due to simple misunderstandings of the UCR burglary definition by uniformed officers. A UCR burglary ordinarily entails the breaking and entering of a *building,* for example, so thefts from covered patios and open garages would not be UCR burglaries. Uniformed officers who are unfamiliar with this fine definitional distinction often report these lesser crimes (e.g., theft, trespass, or vandalism) as UCR burglaries.

(2) *Discretion:* Even when the UCR burglary definition is well understood, its application often requires discretionary decisions of the officer who takes the complaint. Errors may be due to honest differences of opinion as to whether a structure was a garage or a shed, a covered patio or an enclosed porch, and so forth. Discretion may be limited to some extent by the informal policies of beat supervisors. Some beat supervisors, for example, may reward officers who exercise discretion so as to minimize or maximize the burglary count. But in all cases the discretionary component is great.

(3) *Double-counting:* In many circumstances two or more complaint reports are filed for the same incident, and these circumstances lead to double-counting of burglaries.[2] Several days after the burglary, for example, a victim may discover missing items that were not included in the original complaint report. The victim may then call the police, causing a new complaint report to be filed. Few uniformed officers will admit to deliberately processing redundant complaint reports. Officers may not know that a complaint report has already been filed, however, and in some cases, depending on informal beat-level contingencies, may knowingly process redundant reports rather than argue with the victim.

There is no independent measure of these coding errors, but coding clerks report finding several errors each day and, of course, all agree that most errors are never caught. More important, each of these three types of error inflates the UCR burglary rate.

Under the experimental program, the normal complaint-processing flow was changed in two important respects. First, all burglary complaints were investigated. Second, investigations preceded UCR coding decisions, and, as a result, errors in the complaint reports were more likely to be corrected prior to the UCR coding decision. In simplest terms, the program reordered the flow of events by which complaints become recorded in the UCR. The program also reduced the number of personnel filing complaint reports, making the policies on complaint reports more enforceable. Discretionary decisions and double-counting which inflate the UCR burglary rate were minimized. The personnel filing reports, moreover, were experts who appreciated the fine definitional distinctions between UCR burglary, UCR theft, vandalism, trespass, and so forth. Since errors tended to inflate the UCR burglary rate, restructuring of the process affected a reduction in UCR burglaries.

Analysis

To analyze this series, we test the hypothesis that a specific event (investigation of burglary complaints by detectives) caused a change in the time series. Because the change agent is an event, we represent it as a dummy variable or step function:

I_t = 0 prior to the event

= 1 at onset of the event

= 0 at termination of the event and thereafter

The general model for analysis of this time series is written as

$$Y_t = f(I_t) + N_t$$

where N_t is an empirically identified ARIMA noise model and where $f(I_t)$ is some function of the dummy variable, I_t, a so-called "transfer function." The specific function of I_t in this case is

$$f(I_t) = wI_t \qquad \text{and thus}$$
$$Y_t = wI_t + N_t$$

Here w is a scalar parameter to be estimated from the data. Prior to onset of the event, $I_t = 0$, so the expected value of the model is

$$E(Y_t) = 0 + E(N_t)$$

That is, the expected value of the time series, Y_t, is equal to the expected value of an empirically identified ARIMA noise model, N_t. At onset of the event, however, $I_t = 1$, and

$$E(Y_t) = w + E(N_t)$$

That is, the expected value of the time series increases by the quantity w. The parameter w is thus interpreted simply as an increase in the level of the time series due to the intervention.

There are several acceptable methods for identifying the specific form of N_t and estimating the parameter w (see, e.g., McCain and McCleary,

1979; McCleary and Hay, 1980: chap. 3; McDowall et al., 1980). A method that has proved most practical in our experiences, however, is to assume that the N_t component is simple white noise. That is,

$$N_t = a_t \qquad \text{and thus}$$
$$Y_t t = wI_t + a_t$$

Here a_t is a sequence of Normally (Gaussian) and identically distributed independent random shocks; that is,

$$a_t \sim NID(0,\sigma^2)$$

Using an appropriate nonlinear software package (Pack, 1977), we estimate this preliminary model and then examine its residuals to test our assumption that $N_t = a_t$. If this assumption is warranted, successive residuals a_t and a_{t+k} will be uncorrelated. Figure 2.1a shows an estimated autocorrelation function for these residuals. The autocorrelation function at lag-k gives the correlation between a_t and a_{t+k} and, for white noise, we expect all lags to be zero. Since several lags of this autocorrelation function are nonzero, we reject the white noise assumption.[3] Correlated residuals violate a least-squares assumption and result in biased variance estimates. Box-Jenkins-Tiao models attack this problem directly by including serial dependence structures in the model. From the autocorrelation function (Figure 2.1a), it appears that these residuals are distributed as an autoregressive process. We base this identification on the pattern of decay from the first lag of the autocorrelation function, and from this information we respecify N_t as

$$N_t = (1 - \phi_1 B)^{-1} a_t \qquad \text{and thus}$$
$$Y_t = wI_t + (1 - \phi_1 B)^{-1} a_t$$

where B is a backshift operator such that

$$B^n a_t = a_{t-n}$$

While we will not do so here, the expression $(1 - \phi_1 B)^{-1} a_t$ can be expanded as a Taylor series to

$$(1 - \phi_1 B)^{-1} a_t = (1 + \phi_1 B + \phi^2 B^2 + ... + \phi^k Bk + ...)a_t$$
$$= a_t + \phi_1 a_{t-1} + \phi^2 a_{t-2} + ... + \phi^k a_{t-k} + ...$$

The autoregressive parameter ϕ_1 is restricted in absolute value to less than unity. These bounds of stationarity require that ϕ_1 be a fraction and, thus,

GRAPH OF OBSERVED SERIES ACF

```
.+++++++++.+++++++++.+++++++++.+++++++++.+++++++++.+++++++++.+++++++++.+++++++++.
 1                      XXXXXXXXXXXXXXXXXXXXXXXXXXXX          0.58387E+00
 2                      XXXXXXXXXXXXXXXXXXXXXX              0.45797E+00
 3                      XXXXXXXXXXXXXXXX                  0.30314E+00
 4                      XXXXXXXXX                       0.15758E+00
 5                      XXXXXX                          0.92097E-01
 6                XXXXXXX                              -.11770E+00
 7                     XX                               -.16411E-01
 8                      X                                -.14347E-02
 9                     XXX                              -.33474E-01
10                XXXXXXX                              -.11210E+00
11                     XXXX                             -.69736E-01
12                      XX                               0.23186E-01
13                     XXXX                             -.56617E-01
14                     XXXX                             -.50604E-01
15                     XXXX                             -.63550E-01
16                      XXX                              0.30289E-01
17                      XX                               0.10005E-01
18                XXXXXX                               -.10211E+00
19                      XXX                             -.45199E-01
20                      XX                              -.16615E-01
21                      XXX                              0.41172E-01
22                      X                                0.14029E-02
23                      XXX                              0.44030E-01
24                      XXXXXX                           0.10302E+00
25                      XXX                              0.44465E-01
```

Figure 2.1a   The Residual Autocorrelation Function Decays from Its First Lage, Indicating a First-Order Autoregressive Process that the infinite series converge to zero. The N_t component of our model, in other words, consists of a current random shock, a_t, and an infinite series of weighted past shocks. The weights applied to past shocks decrease geometrically, however, imitating the geometric decay evidenced in the first few lags of the autocorrelation function.

Using the same nonlinear software package, we estimate the parameters of this new model and, again, examine the residual autocorrelation function (Figure 2.1b). If this model is appropriate, we expect the autocorrelation function to have no statistically significant spikes, but, as shown, there are significant correlations at the sixth and twelfth (and perhaps eighteenth) lags. To accommodate the apparent seasonality, we specify an autoregressive parameter of the sixth order. Our tentative model is thus

$$Y_t = wI_t + (1 - \phi_1 B - \phi_6 B^6)^{-1} a_t$$

Using the same nonlinear software package, we estimate the parameters of this model as

$\phi_1 = .63704$ with t-statistic = 7.14

$\phi_6 = -.50218$ with t-statistic = -4.24

$w = -200.20$ with t-statistic = -11.14

The residual autocorrelation function from this model (not shown) has no statistically significant spikes, indicating that the model is appropriate for this time series. Since all parameters of this model are statistically significant and since its residuals are not different from white noise, the modeling procedure is completed. The substantive implications of this model are straightforward. Prior to intervention, the series fluctuated around a mean level (of approximately 700 UCR burglaries per month) as first- and sixth-order autoregressive process. With onset of the intervention, the mean series level dropped by more than 200 UCR burglaries per month. Then with termination of the intervention, the mean series level returned to its preintervention "normal" state. Moreover, the shift in level due to this intervention was statistically different from zero.

CASE 2:
HIERARCHICAL CONTROL

Figure 2.2 shows monthly UCR burglaries for City B, another large southwestern city, from January 1975 to May 1981. Prior to July 1979, this series follows a slight downward trend. Thereafter, the series rises dramatically. Total UCR burglaries for the last six months of 1979 are 20

```
      GRAPH OF OBSERVED SERIES ACF
      .+++++++++.+++++++++.+++++++++.+++++++++.+++++++++.+++++++++.+++++++++.+++++++++.+++++++++.+++++++++.
  1                                      XXXXXXX                                                   -.11020E+00
  2                                            XXXXXXXX                                            0.14582E+00
  3                                            XXXX                                                0.69660E-01
  4                                           XX                                                   -.20401E-01
  5                                            XXXXXXXXX                                           0.15621E+00
  6                             XXXXXXXXXXXXXXXX                                                   -.30058E+00
  7                                            XXXXX                                               0.74073E-01
  8                                            XXX                                                 0.35890E-01
  9                                            XX                                                  0.15381E-01
 10                                     XXXXXXXX                                                   -.14373E+00
 11                                         XXXXX                                                  -.76786E-01
 12                                            XXXXXXXXX                                           0.15030E+00
 13                                        XXXXXX                                                  -.10645E+00
 14                                            X                                                   -.40019E-02
 15                                      XXXXXXX                                                   -.12387E+00
 16                                            XXXXXX                                              0.90687E-01
 17                                            XXXXX                                               0.81547E-01
 18                                   XXXXXXXXXX                                                   -.18364E+00
 19                                            XX                                                  0.10326E-01
 20                                          XXX                                                   -.34098E-01
 21                                            XXXXXX                                              0.90884E-01
 22                                         XXXXX                                                  -.78567E-01
 23                                            X                                                   -.52472E-02
 24                                            XXXXXXXX                                            0.13094E+0C
 25                                            XX                                                  0.22030E-01
```

Figure 2.1b The Residual Autocorrelation Function Decays from Its Sixth Lag, Indicating the Need for a Sixth-Order Autoregressive Process

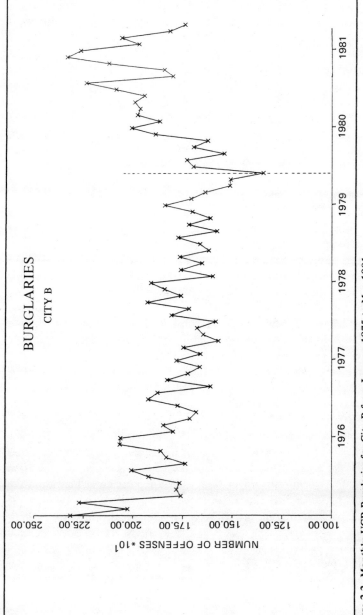

BURGLARIES
CITY B

Figure 2.2 Monthly UCR Burglaries for City B from January 1975 to May 1981

NOTE: Vertical dotted line indicates the month in which an incumbent chief resigned.

percent higher than the total for the first six months. The most obvious explanation for the increase in UCR burglaries shown in Figure 2.2 is that "real" crime increased correspondingly. But our data support another explanation. Onset of this UCR "crime wave" coincided with retirement of an incumbent police chief. The administrative shakeup which followed the retirement had a direct effect on the UCR Coding Bureau, as the results in Figure 2.2 show.

In a study of "getting the crime rate down," Seidman and Couzens (1974) focused on the discretionary decisions of patrol officers. Given discretion at the street level, a police chief can "wish" crime rates down by rewarding district commanders who produce low UCR rates; they in turn can pass this "wish" down the ranks until it reaches the patrol officer. Hierarchical control of street-level discretion is essential to this process; and, of course, when hierarchical control breaks down, crime rates rise. In this case, four of the five incumbent assistant chiefs were replaced by the incoming administration. Because these exempted positions were filled from within, the retirement had a domino effect, resulting in as many as three dozen personnel changes at and above the rank of captain.

In this case, one need not focus on street-level discretion to explain the increase in official crime rates. The UCR Coding Bureau was not immune from the domino effect. The Coding Bureau staff, three officers and four civilians, were supervised by a sergeant. The sergeant reported to the commander of the Research and Planning Division, who in turn reported to an assistant chief. As the administrative shakeup ensued, the assistant chief, commander, and sergeant were all replaced.

The breakdown in hierarchical authority during the summer of 1979 had real implications for the coding of UCR crimes. When the commander left, the sergeant began to make decisions that had previously been made by the commander. When the sergeant was replaced a few months later, the disintegration process continued. UCR coding clerks began to make decisions that had previously been made by the sergeant. Coding decisions for UCR burglaries seldom reduce to mechanical applications of written guidelines. As demonstrated in Case 1, field reports do not always make facts clear. Crimes that appear to fit the UCR burglary definition on the basis of field reports are often better categorized as "no crime," theft, vandalism, or trespass. Since UCR coding decisions always involve discretion, even a slight change in the decision-making process can result in a profound increase in a UCR rate. The increase shown in Figure 2.2 represents a change of only two or three UCR burglaries per day, and this is well within the range one could expect from a slight change in the decision-making process.

The genesis of this "crime wave" is not unlike several others reported in the literature. In Chicago (Campbell, 1969; Glass et al., 1975), Kansas City

(Guyot, 1976), and Washington, D.C. (Seidman and Couzens, 1974), changes in police department administrations led to changes in hierarchical authority. The precise nature of change in each case was idiosyncratic and hence unpredictable. Nevertheless, since crime rates were controlled by means of hierarchical control, the changes in structure led to changes in UCR rates. The facts in this case are entirely consistent with the literature, although, as noted, we trace the cause directly to the disintegration of authority in the UCR coding unit.

Analysis

Analysis of this UCR burglary series uncovers an important aspect of this phenomenon. In Case 1, complaint-processing was restructured abruptly and we expected to find an abrupt drop in UCR burglaries. In Case 2, on the other hand, the time series did not change abruptly with the chief's retirement, but instead increased gradually to reflect the gradual disintegration of a hierarchical authority structure. Reflecting this gradual impact, we require a more complicated $f(I_t)$.

$$f(I_t) = (1 - dB)^{-1} w I_t$$

Assuming a white noise process, our tentative model is

$$Y_t = (1 - dB)^{-1} w I_t + a_t$$

To illustrate the dynamics of this model, suppose that the intervention (retirement of the incumbent chief in this case) occurs at time $t = i$. Then prior to the intervention, $I_t = 0$ and the expected value of the model is zero. But then at $t = i$, $I_i = 1$ and

$$Y_i = (1 - dB)^{-1} w I_i$$

As was true of the autoregressive operator in the preceding analysis, the expression $(1 - dB)^{-1}$ may be expanded as a Taylor series. Substituting the infinite series, the model is rewritten as

$$Y_i = w I_i + d w I_{i-1} + d^2 w I_{i-2} + ... + d^k w I_{i-k} + ...$$

Now since all values of I_t are equal to zero prior to $t = i$, only the first element of this infinite series is nonzero and thus

$$Y_i = w$$

In the next observation, $I_{i+1} = 1$, and

$$Y_{i+1} = wI_i{+}1 + dwI_i + d^2 wI_{i-1} + ... + d^k wI_{i-1-k}$$

Since I_{i-1} through I_{i-1-k} are zero, only the first two terms of this series are nonzero and thus

$$Y_{i+1} = w + dw$$

Following this same logic, successive postintervention observations are expected to be

$$Y_{i+2} = w + dw + d^2 w$$
$$Y_{i+3} = w + dw + d^2 w + d^3 w$$

•

$$Y_{i+k} = w + dw + d^2 w + d^3 w + ... + d^k w$$

Now if the parameter d is constrained in absolute value to less than unity, the infinite series converges to zero. Thus, although the level of the series increases with each postintervention observation, successive increments grow smaller. We will illustrate this property of the model after our analysis.

Figure 2.2a shows the residual autocorrelation function estimated under an assumption that N_t is a white noise process. Since there are several statistically significant values in the autocorrelation function, we reject a white noise model for these residuals. Although this autocorrelation function is somewhat ambiguous, it decays from its first lag, suggesting an autoregressive process. Our tentative model is thus

$$Y_t = (1 - dB)^{-1} wI_t + (1 - \phi_1 B)^{-1} a_t$$

This is the same N_t we initially identified in the preceding analysis. The parameter estimates for this model are

ϕ_1 = .47303 with t-statistic = 4.20

d   = .90382 with t-statistic = 4.33

w = 26.930 with t-statistic = 1.68

The residual autocorrelation function for this model (not shown) has no statistically significant values, indicating that the model is appropriate.

To interpret this model, we note that the expected value of a_t is zero and hence that the expected value of the time series is $f(I_t)$ plus the series

GRAPH OF OBSERVED SERIES ACF

```
  .++++++++.++++++++.++++++++.++++++++.++++++++.++++++++.++++++++.++++++++.++++++++.
 1   XXXXXXXXXXXXXXXXXXXXX                                                      0.42217E+00
 2   XXXXXXXXX                                                                  0.19169E+00
 3   XXXXXXX                                                                    0.14169E+00
 4   XXXXXX                                                                     0.12259E+00
 5   XXXXXXXXXXXXXXX                                                            0.29233E+00
 6   XXXXX                                                                      0.96196E-01
 7   XXXXXXXXXXXX                                                               0.25449E+00
 8   XXX                                                                        0.34367E-01
 9   XX                                                                         0.12388E-01
10   XXXXXXX                                                                    0.13101E+00
11   XXXX                                                                       0.57701E-01
12   XXXXXXXXXX                                                                 0.19026E+00
13   XXXXXX                                                                    -.93576E-01
14   XXXX                                                                      -.62604E-01
15   XXXX                                                                      -.50401E-01
16   XXXX                                                                      -.52440E-01
17   XXXX                                                                       0.58073E-01
18   XXXXXXXX                                                                  -.14032E+00
19   XXX                                                                       -.39527E-01
20   XXXXXXX                                                                   -.12897E+00
21   XXXXX                                                                     -.77916E-01
22   XXXX                                                                       0.61119E-01
23   XXX                                                                        0.48698E-01
24   XXXXXXXXX                                                                  0.16225E+00
25   XXX                                                                       -.31097E-01
```

Figure 2.2a   The Residual Autocorrelation Function Decays from Its First Lag, Indicating a First-Order Autoregressive Process

27

mean. Prior to intervention, the series fluctuates about its mean level (approximately 1750 UCR burglaries per month) as a first-order autoregressive process. With onset of the intervention, the series mean begins to rise. Successive postintervention increments over the "normal" preintervention mean are

$$Y_i = w$$
$$= 26.93$$
$$Y_{i+1} = w + dw$$
$$= 26.93 + (.90382)(26.93)$$
$$= 26.94 + 24.34 = 51.28$$
$$Y_{i+2} = w + dw + d^2w$$
$$= 26.93 + (.90382)(26.93) + (.90382)^2(26.93)$$
$$= 26.93 + 24.34 + 21.97 = 73.25$$
$$Y_{i+3} = w + dw + d^2w + d^3w$$
$$= 26.93 + (.90328)(26.93) + (.90328)^2(26.93) + (.90328)^3$$
$$(26.93)(26.93)$$
$$= 26.93 + 24.34 + 21.97 + 19.85 = 93.10$$

and so forth. The series level increases throughout the postintervention period, but successive increments grow smaller and smaller, converging to zero. Given this convergence, the asymptotic or "steady state" level may be evaluated as

$$\text{Asymptotic level} = \frac{26.93}{1 - .90382} = 280$$

In other words, the postintervention series approaches 280 UCR burglaries as a limit. The rate at which the series approaches its asymptotic level is determined by the value of d. When d is large, as it is in this example, the asymptotic level is realized slowly. When d is small, on the other hand, near zero, the asymptotic level is realized quite rapidly. And of course, when d = 0, the asymptotic level is realized instantaneously (as was the case in our preceding analysis). The parameter d in this sense is interpreted literally as the rate at which the series level responds to an intervention.

As a final point, we note that the parameter w is significant only at a .10 level. If we required a higher level of significance, say .05, we would have to conclude that the impact of the intervention in this example was not statistically different from zero.

CASE 3: PROTECTION AND FRONT-END SCREENING

The literature describes two distinct types of unreported crime. The first type consists of crimes which, for whatever reason, citizens do not report to the police. Skogan (1976) estimates that over 50 percent of all serious crimes are unreported in this sense. A second type of "unreported" crime consists of crimes which citizens report to the police but which, for whatever reason, the police refuse to count as "real" crimes (Black, 1970; Waegel, 1981). The literature gives us no measure of the proportion of total crime which falls into this second category, but it is undoubtedly a significant proportion.

There is no clear understanding of the factors which underlie this phenomenon, but one obvious factor is the nature of the initial dispatching action. Pepinsky (1976; see also, Maxfield, 1981) has shown, for example, that patrolmen are most likely to report an incident as a crime when the dispatcher designates the call as a crime. In light of this, as a third principle, we suggest that UCR rates will be a function of dispatching routines and, in particular, the UCR reports will increase as dispatched "calls for service" increase. The interesting question, of course, is which organizational structures affect the rate at which citizen complaints are dispatched as "calls for service."

Figure 2.3 shows monthly "calls for service" dispatched by the City A Police Department. A "service call" for our purposes is a citizen call for assistance which results in the dispatch of an officer to the scene. Any official crime (Part I UCR or otherwise) must begin with a service call, but, of course, not all service calls result in an official crime. And if a call for police assistance does not result in dispatch of an officer, the event is not a service call. This is an important point because, clearly, a police department can increase or decrease its official crime rate by increasing or decreasing the likelihood that a call for assistance will result in a dispatched "service call."

Prior to April 1979, all shifts in the City A Dispatch Bureau were supervised by sergeants. Thereafter, sergeants were removed from most shifts. The result of this administrative change was an increase in the number of "service calls" dispatched and, as Black et al. would argue, an increase in crime due to a decrease in "unreported" crime. Judging from the effect shown in Figure 2.3, the proportion of "unreported" crime in City A is relatively large—perhaps 20 percent or higher.

Our interpretation of this phenomenon rests on an understanding of the work performed by dispatchers. Dispatchers write records, answer telephones (sometimes), and, if necessary, dispatch officers to answer citizen calls for assistance.[4] Sending officers to the scene is a decisionary task, but

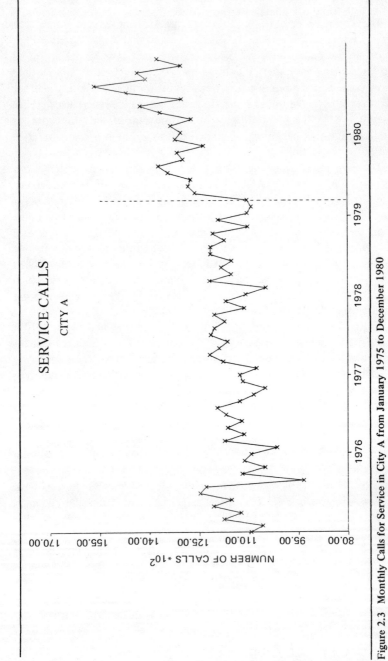

Figure 2.3 Monthly Calls for Service in City A from January 1975 to December 1980

NOTE: Vertical dotted line indicates the month in which sergeants were removed from supervisory positions in the Dispatch Bureau.

only a small proportion of decisions involve real discretion. More than half of the calls to the Dispatch Bureau, for example, are "wrong numbers," such as requests for nonpolice services (sanitation, public health, etc.) and requests for general information. Other calls report threats to safety, such as crimes in progress or public disturbances. The decision in both of these cases is obvious.

In some cases, however, the decision is not obvious and the dispatcher must exercise discretion. The most theoretically interesting cases involve incidents that may be "crimes" in a technical sense but that nevertheless are deemed questionable. Many calls for assistance on "auto thefts," for example, turn out to be repossessions or towaways of illegally parked cars. Calls reporting "burglaries" or "thefts" may similarly turn out to be civil matters, such as property disputes among divorcing spouses. There is no apparent threat to public safety in any of these examples. More important, these "crimes" are marginal or unimportant. They are not "real crimes" in the way police officers understand that term. This is an important aspect of the phenomenon. As uniformed officers, the sergeants made normal distinctions between real crimes and complaints that appeared not to be real crimes. Dispatchers were encouraged to handle the latter events with some action other than sending officers to the scene.

When the sergeants were removed from the Dispatch Bureau, however, the dispatchers reverted to a more formal, bureaucratized system. The validity of a call was not questioned. Officers were sent to the scene of all calls. Many calls for police assistance may not be wholly valid, of course, at least from the perspective of the street-wise sergeants. Sending officers to answer such calls wastes resources, but dispatchers are rewarded only for seeing that calls are answered, not for conserving resources. By sending officers on all calls, the dispatchers protected themselves, optimizing personal rewards and minimizing personal risks, but at the expense of departmental resources.

Analysis

In this case, we assume that the series will respond instantaneously to the intervention. Our tentative model then is

$$Y_t = wI_t + a_t$$

The residual autocorrelation function estimated for this model, shown in Figure 2.3a, has statistically significant values at the first, second, sixth, twelfth, and eighteenth lags (the spike at the twenty-fourth lag is not quite significant). In preceding analyses, the autocorrelation function decayed,

GRAPH OF OBSERVED SERIES ACF

```
 .++++++++.++++++++.++++++++.++++++++.++++++++.++++++++.++++++++.++++++++.++++++++.++++++++.

 1                    xxxxxxxxxxxxx                          0.25740E+00
 2                    xxxxxxxxxxxxx                          0.25698E+00
 3                    xxxxxxxxx                              0.16269E+00
 4                   xx                                     -.28264E-01
 5                    xxxx                                   0.56069E-01
 6       xxxxxxxxxxxxxxxxx                                  -.33347E+00
 7                 xxx                                      -.37613E-01
 8               xxxxxx                                     -.10500E+00
 9                xxxx                                      -.59735E-01
10                 xxx                                      -.45897E-01
11              xxxxx                                       -.89731E-01
12                    xxxxxxxxxxxxx                          0.25866E+00
13                 x                                        -.17156E-02
14                    xx                                     0.26567E-01
15             xxxxxxxx                                     -.13015E+00
16            xxxxxxxx                                      -.15293E+00
17            xxxxxx                                        -.12840E+00
18      xxxxxxxxxxxxxxxxxxx                                 -.36020E+00
19            xxxxxxxx                                      -.16693E+00
20            xxxxxxxxx                                     -.16796E+00
21                  xx                                      -.23531E-01
22                  xx                                      -.19065E-01
23                xxx                                       -.44088E-01
24                    xxxxxxxxxxx                            0.20199E+00
25                    xx                                     0.15746E-01
```

Figure 2.3a The Residual Autocorrelation Funcition Has Discrete Spikes at the First, Second, Sixth, Twelfth, and Eighteenth Lags

NOTE: Discrete spikes indicate moving average structures at these lags.

suggesting an autoregressive model for N_t. In this analysis, however, we see discrete spikes which indicate a moving average structure. Moving average parameters generally remove discrete spikes from the autocorrelation function while autoregressive parameters remove a series of (geometrically decaying) spikes from the autocorrelation function. Our tentative model is thus

$$Y_t = wI_t + (1 - \theta_1 B - \theta_2 B^2 - \theta_6 B^6 - \theta_{12} B^{12} - \theta_{18} B^{18}) at$$

Parameter estimates for this model are

θ_1 = $-.25218$ with t-statistic = -2.73

θ_2 = $-.16029$ with t-statistic = -2.08

θ_6 = $.21401$ with t-statistic = 3.02

θ_{12} = $-.23561$ with t-statistic = -3.53

θ_{18} = $.77796$ with t-statistic = 12.95

w = 1965.9 with t-statistic = 11.87

The residual autocorrelation function (not shown) has no statistically significant values, so we accept this model for the service calls time series. Our interpretation of the model is that prior to the intervention, service calls fluctuated about a mean level (approximately 12,000 service calls per month) as an eighteenth-order moving average. When the sergeants were removed from supervisory positions, however, the mean series level increased by 1965.9 monthly calls. Finally, the increase is statistically significant.

The sergeants acted as a screening structure at the front end of the complaint-processing system. Screening has no direct effect on UCR coding decisions, of course, but when a call goes unanswered, a UCR crime cannot result. If the call does represent a UCR crime, it goes unreported. When an officer is sent to the call, on the other hand, there is an unknown but nonzero probability that a UCR crime will result. Increasing the number of "calls for service" by removing the informal screening mechanism is thus expected to increase the rate of such UCR crimes as burglary, larceny, and auto theft. UCR crime in City A did increase substantially during this period, and the police department interpreted this as an increase in real crime. Our alternative interpretation is more plausible, however: Calls for service increased when sergeants were removed from the Dispatch Bureau. The rate at which crimes were reported increased but not as a result of an increase in real crime.

CONCLUSION

This essay has demonstrated the utility of time series methods, particularly the time series quasi-experiment, for analyzing the relationship between organizational structure and official crime rates. The conventional wisdom is that UCR statistics are so unreliable as to be useless for research. Seidman and Couzens (1974: 463) argue, for example, that "crime statistics are basically non-comparable across jurisdictions," and hence, that cross-sectional analyses of UCR statistics are not possible. Despite this gloomy overstatement of the conventional wisdom, they are widely used in criminological research. Our findings support the conventional view on one level. Any researcher who analyzed these series without knowing about the interventions would arrive at nonsense conclusions. But on another level, our findings support a more sanguine view. Since each of our three cases involves a clearly defined organizational variable, research into the structural determinants of official crime rates, as originally suggested by Kitsuse and Cicourel, is promising.

Any organizational outcome theory of crime rates must begin with a model of the organizational process. A simple model which, in our opinion, describes most large-city police departments is

Complaint $\rightarrow$ Investigation $\rightarrow$ Coding Decision

(Input)   (Output)

The process is initiated by a citizen complaint, and any organizational facet that affects the propensity of citizens to seek police assistance is called a "screen." Because system outputs are proportional to inputs, screening structures that reduce the level of inputs, making it harder for citizens to complain, reduce the official crime rate.

Our third case illustrates a typical screening structure. Sergeants in one police department dispatch bureau routinely screened complaints that they understood to be "marginal." It is not surprising that the sergeants relied on complainant characteristics, especially race, to calculate the expected marginality of a complaint. Complaints from ghetto areas were heavily screened and were less likely to result in dispatched service calls.

The basis of this phenomenon is a conflict between public perceptions and the street cop ethos (Black, 1970; Wilson, 1975). While the nature of screening may vary from case to case, we expect the degree of screening to be a function of how strongly the process reflects a street cop ethos. In particular, where the dispatch function is controlled by street cops, we expect a vigorous screening structure.

Complaints that pass through the screening structure are investigated. Our first case illustrates the differences between a general investigation, conducted by patrol officers, and a specific investigation conducted by detectives. Specific investigations are relatively more bureaucratized than general investigations. Detectives may not be more adept at investigation than patrol officers, but they are certainly more adept at applying formal definitions to cases. The effect of mandating specific investigations of all burglary complaints in City A was an increase in the reliability of UCR coding decisions (evidenced by a decrease in the monthly variance); and because coding decision errors tended to inflate the UCR count, a decrease in the UCR burglary rate. Generalizing this result, we expect official crime rates to vary inversely with the relative use of formal, specific investigation.

Finally, given the specified effects of screening and investigation, the official crime rate will be a function of organizational goals. In our second case, retirement of an incumbent police chief led to an increase in UCR burglaries. The general principle here is that police departments have abstract goals operationalized in terms of a crime rate. To achieve its goals, however, the department must be able to exercise hierarchical control over its complaint processors and, *ceteris paribus,* the more effective the hierarchical organizational structure, the lower the UCR crime rate.

A minimal theory of crime rates as organizational outcomes requires a cross-sectional study of dependent variable crime rates explained by three independent structural variables. The theory is not easily tested, however. An obvious weakness is that not all relationships are fully specified. For screening structures, the relationship is clear: Screening reduces the official crime rate, especially UCR assaults, auto thefts, burglaries, and larcenies. But for investigative structures, the relationship is more complex. While investigative structures reduced the UCR burglary rate in City A, these structures could increase the UCR burglary rate in other cities or under other circumstances. Elaborating on this point, any theory must recognize three possible process outcomes. After screening, a citizen complaint may result in an official crime or not; but a complaint of a specific crime, such as burglary, may also be displaced or downgraded to a nonburglary category such as theft, vandalism, or trespass. We suspect that investigative structures are more likely to displace complaints than to divert them entirely. Finally, for hierarchical control structures, we cannot assume that all police departments follow the same simple-minded goal of reducing crime rates across the board. Goals are more likely to be operationalized as complicated mixtures of increases, decreases, and displacements.

Lacking adequate specification, we could agree with the conventional view that UCR statistics are "basically noncomparable" across jurisdictions; or at least that there is no theoretical basis for their comparison. Given the relatively constant nature of "structures," longitudinal analyses appear to be more valid, but this may be only an appearance. In either case, we advise a return to the understanding that UCR data are "official statistics" which may be used validly only for the study of organizational processes (Kitsuse and Cicourel, 1963). Research following this tradition must emphasize qualitative studies of single departments. Clearly, we are not yet at the stage where theory will support broad statistical generalizations across many departments.

NOTES

1. We regularly visited these police departments in various official and unofficial capacities during a two-year period. The conclusions summarized here are based on participant observation and interview data reported in McCleary et al. (1982). See that work for a more complete description of these phenomena.

2. Ann L. Schneider (personal correspondence) has discovered a undercounting phenomenon for apartment burglaries in a large city. In cases where several apartments are burglarized, a single report is filed with the apartment manager listed as complainant. UCR coding clerks incorrectly counted the several burglaries as one UCR burglary.

3. For the three series analyzed here, an autocorrelation will be statistically significant at a level greater than .05 if it is larger than .22 in absolute value. Our analyses follow the procedures described in McCleary and Hay (1980; McDowall et al., 1980). The reader who is totally unfamiliar with these procedures may consult either source for a more complete introduction.

4. In most large cities, dispatching work is divided into two distinct functions. Phone calls are answered by operators, who forward all action requests for service to dispatchers. Operators are typically civilian employees and dispatchers are typically uniformed officers, but both are supervised by the sergeant. See Antunes and Scott (1981) for an excellent description of dispatching.

REFERENCES

ANTUNES, G. and E. J. SCOTT (1981) "Calling the cops: police telephone operators and citizen calls for service." J. of Criminal Justice 9: 165-179.

BLACK, D. J. (1970) "Production of crime rates." Amer. Soc. Rev. 35: 733-747.

BOX, G.E.P. and G. M. JENKINS (1976) Time Series Analysis: Forecasting and Control. San Francisco: Holden-Day.

BOX, G.E.P. and G. C. TIAO (1975) "Intervention analysis with applications to economic and environmental problems." J. of the Amer. Statistical Assoc. 70: 70-92.

——— (1965) "A change in level of a nonstationary time series." Biometrika 52: 181-192.

CAMPBELL, D. T. (1969) "Reforms as experiments." Amer. Psychologist 24: 409-429.

——— and J. C. STANLEY (1966) Experimental and Quasi-Experimental Designs for Research. Chicago: Rand McNally.

GLASS, G. V, V. L. WILLSON, and J. M. GOTTMAN (1975) The Design and Analysis of Time Series Experiments. Boulder: Colorado Associated Univ. Press.

GUYOT, D. (1976) "What productivity? What bargain?" Public Admin. Rev. 36: 341.

HINDELANG, M. J. (1976) Criminal Victimization in Eight American Cities: A Descriptive Analysis of Common Theft and Assault. Cambridge, MA: Ballinger.

KITSUSE, J. I. and A. V. CICOUREL (1963) "A note on the use of official statistics." Social Problems 11: 131-138.

MAXFIELD, M. G. (1981) "Service time, dispatch time, and demand for police services: helping more by serving less." School of Public and Environmental Affairs, Indiana University.

——— D. A. LEWIS and R. SZOC (1980) "Producing official crimes: verified crime reports as measures of police output." Social Sci. Q. 61: 221-236.

McCAIN, L. J. and R. McCLEARY (1979) "The statistical analysis of the simple interrupted time series quasi-experiment," chap. 6 in T. D. Cook and D. T. Campbell (eds.) Quasi-Experimentation: Design and Analysis Issues for Field Settings. Chicago: Rand McNally.

McCLEARY, R. and R. A. HAY, Jr. (1980) Applied Time Series Analysis for the Social Sciences. Beverly Hills, CA: Sage.

——— B. C. NIENSTEDT, and J. M. ERVEN (1982) "Uniform Crime Reports as organizational outcomes: three time series quasi-experiments." Social Problems 29.

McDOWALL, D., R. McCLEARY, E. E. MEIDINGER, and R. A. HAY (1980) Interrupted Time Series Analysis. Beverly Hills, CA: Sage.

PACK, D. J. (1977) A Computer Program for Analysis of Time Series Models Using the Box-Jenkins Philosophy. Hatboro, PA: Automatic Forecasting Service.

PEPINSKY, H. (1976) "Police patrolmen's offense-reporting behavior." J. of Research in Crime and Delinquency 13: 33-47.

SIEDMAN, D. and M. COUZENS (1974) "Getting the crime rate down: political pressure and crime reporting." Law and Society Rev. 8: 457-493.

SKOGAN, W. G. (1976) "Crime and crime rates," pp. 105-120 in Sample Surveys of the Victims of Crime. Cambridge, MA: Ballinger.

——— (1974) "The validity of official crime statistics: an empirical investigation." Social Sci. Q. 54: 25-38.

WAEGEL, W. B. (1981) "Case routinization in investigative police work." Social Problems 28: 261-275.

WILSON, J. Q. (1975) Varieties of Police Behavior. New York: Basic Books.

3

Richard A. Berk
David Rauma

University of California, Santa Barbara

Sheldon L. Messinger

University of California, Berkeley

A FURTHER TEST OF THE STABILITY
OF PUNISHMENT HYPOTHESIS

Durkheimian views on the nature of social control (1964a, 1964b) have led some scholars to assert that societies are characterized by stable levels of punishment. In the absence of social upheavals, the proportion over time of people sanctioned through "repressive law" should closely approximate some constant fraction of the society's population. Probably the strongest support for this "stability of punishment" hypothesis lies in the work of Alfred Blumstein and his colleagues (Blumstein and Cohen, 1973; Blumstein et al., 1977; Blumstein and Moitra, 1979), but at this juncture the overall weight of evidence is equivocal. A growing number of studies have criticized directly the earlier stability of punishment research and/or failed to find stable levels of punishment when new data sets are examined (Waller and Chan, 1977; Greenberg, 1977, 1980; Cahalan, 1979; Rauma, 1981). Moreover, in probably the most thorough formulation and test of the stability of punishment hypothesis, Berk, Rauma, Messinger, and Cooley (1981) find the Durkheimian perspective particularly wanting.

While the work of Berk, Rauma, Messinger, and Cooley (hereafter referred to as BRMC) raises some rather fundamental questions about the stability of punishment hypothesis as usually articulated, there are a wide variety of ways to conceptualize punishment. Indeed, BRMC suggest that

AUTHORS' NOTE: Thanks go to Nancy Blum for helping collect the budget data. Support for this research was provided by the National Science Foundation.

one fruitful alternative might lie in "monetizing" the relevant variables. Thus, the hypothesized stable ratio might be better approached as the amount of money spent on punishment over the total spent on all other public expenditures. That is, there is some constant relationship between how much money is spent on punishment compared to how much is spent on other public services. At the very least, a monetized formulation is fully consistent with the growing criminal justice literature produced by economists (e.g., Becker, 1968; Stigler, 1970; Votey and Phillips, 1973) and with what is known about the real politik of criminal justice (e.g., Berk et al., 1977). In addition, there is some evidence that even preindustrial societies took the costs of punishment into account (Perry, 1980; Ruggiero, 1980) through the tradeoffs between incarcerating large numbers of the underclasses and maintaining an adequate local source of labor and military recruits. In short, although monetizing the stability of punishment hypothesis is but one of many options, it is one that has some face validity: Punishment is a cost not only to the offender but to the greater society. The question, then, is whether these costs might play some role in the amount of punishment a society delivers. Is there some relatively stable balance between how much a society is prepared to pay for punishing its criminals and how much society is prepared to pay for other public services?

In this chapter, therefore, we examine the traditional stability of punishment hypothesis and more general equilibrating formulations consistent with the spirit of Durkheim's views on the functioning of repressive law, but with a monetized measure of punishment. In that effort, we will draw heavily on the models first introduced by BRMC. We will then estimate the parameters of these models, relying primarily on the BRMC data set: yearly data for the state of California from 1860 to 1970. Tests will follow for the viability of "monetized equilibration." Finally, the implications of the tests will be considered for what they suggest about future research questions.

AN EQUILIBRATING MODEL OF PUNISHMENT

It may not be reading too much into Durkheim to concur with Blumstein and his colleagues (hereafter referred to as Blumstein) that Durkheim's views on the stability of punishment require some kind of underlying, dynamic process. By "dynamic" we mean nothing more than that, in contrast to static models where an endogenous variable(s) is taken as a function of a set of regressors at the same point in time, there are "non-contemporaneous relationships between the variables" (Harvey, 1981: 221). To take a very simple example, the number of people incarcerated in a given year might be a function of the unemployment rate the year before, and/or a function of the number of people incarcerated in the previous year (i.e., a lagged endogenous variable).

Equally important, the Durkeimian perspective almost certainly requires an "error correction mechanism" (Harvey, 1981: 288-292). As Blumstein and Cohen (1973: 200) note,

> there are a variety of processes in the society which operate to maintain a constant level of punishment, and this level adapts to changing levels of actual crimes. . . . Under this hypothesis, if behavior were to become less deviant through a decrease in the occurrence of infractions, . . . then the society would respond according to Durkheim's model by re-defining previously minor infractions as crimes, and punishing these. The result would be the stable maintenance of a reasonable amount of punishment.

In other words, there is some target level of punishment, and deviations from the target set in motion social processes that make the proper corrections.

These and other considerations discussed by BRMC lead naturally to a difference equation framework (e.g., Chiang, 1974: 549-621; Goldberg, 1958) resting on rational polynomial functions of the following form:

$$A(L)\ln(Y_t) = B(L)\ln(X_t) + C(L)\ln(U_t) \qquad [1]$$

where $A(L)$, $B(L)$, and $C(L)$ are polynomials, and L is the lag operator. Y is some endogenous variable, X is some exogenous variable, and U is a stochastic disturbance. Equation 1 can be complicated by adding other regressors, but the single regressor form will suffice for now. It is also possible to consider more than one endogenous variable, within a multiple equation framework (e.g., Chiang, 1974: 602-611), but we will leave that for some other time. Finally, all of the variables are in natural logarithms, which allows one, under certain conditions, to specify causal models in growth rates (Theil, 1978: 188-191). Indeed, we will rely heavily on such formulations below.

MODEL I:
A CORRECTING MECHANISM
WITH A FIXED TARGET

Equation 2 shows a relatively simply rational polynomial function with two generic variables: corrections expenditures in a given year, C_t, and all other state expenditures in a particular jurisdiction in the same year, S_t.

$$(1-\gamma L)\ln(C_t) = (\delta_1 + \delta_2 L)\ln(S_t) + \ln(a_t) \qquad [2]$$

Equation 2 indicates that corrections expenditures are a linear function of all other state expenditures plus a random disturbance. Why such relationships might exist and why there are three parameters and two lag operators at this juncture are not important. In any case, equation 2 is hardly the end of the story. Consider the following manipulations.

$$[\ln(C_t) - \ln(C_{t-1})] = (\gamma - 1)\ln(C_{t-1}) + \delta_1 \ln(S_t) + \delta_2 \ln(S_{t-1}) + \ln(a_t) \qquad [3a]$$

$$= \delta_3 \ln(C_{t-1}) + \delta_1 \ln(S_t) + \delta_2 \ln(S_{t-1}) + \ln(a_t)$$

$$= \delta_3 \ln(C_{t-1}) + \delta_1 \ln(S_t) - \delta_1 \ln(S_{t-1}) - \delta_3 \ln(S_{t-1}) + \ln(a_t)$$

$$\ln\left(\frac{C_t}{C_{t-1}}\right) = \delta_1 \ln\left(\frac{S_t}{S_{t-1}}\right) + \delta_3 \ln\left(\frac{C_{t-1}}{S_{t-1}}\right) + \ln(a_t) \qquad [3b]$$

Beginning with equation 3a, a lagged value of the endogenous variable is subtracted from both sides of the equation, the terms are rearranged, and, for ease of exposition, δ_3 is introduced in place of $(\gamma - 1)$. Then, if one adds the constraint that $\delta_1 + \delta_2 + \delta_3 = 0$ and substitutes $-\delta_1 - \delta_3$ for δ_2, one obtains, after rearranging, equation 3b. In other words, 3b is a restricted version of equation 2, based on the restriction that the sum of the parameters in equation 2 equals zero.

While the restriction perhaps seems simple and uninteresting, it actually produces the kind of dynamic, self-correcting formulation we are seeking. First, equation 3b indicates that the growth rate in corrections expenditures is a linear function of the growth rate of other state expenditures in the same year. To this we would add that the regression coefficient is probably positive: The growth in corrections expenditures increases (decreases) when the growth in all other state expenditures increases (decreases). In other words, corrections expenditures are carried along with an overall increase in the cost of state services.

Second, the corrections expenditures growth rate is a linear function of the log-ratio of corrections expenditures to other state expenditures, both lagged by one year (if the time units are years). The key to its role, however, lies in its regression coefficient. If the relationship shown in equation 2 is stable (Chiang, 1974: 558-562),[1] then γ must be less than 1.0 in absolute value. It follows that the regression coefficient associated with the log-ratio must be negative (but greater than -2.0). This implies that when the ratio of corrections expenditures relative to other expenditures is too high, the corrections expenditures growth rate will decline. When the ratio of corrections expenditures to other expenditures is too low, the corrections expenditures growth rate will increase. Thus, the log-ratio serves are an "error-correcting mechanism."

Putting together the role of the growth rate of other state expenditures and the log-ratio of corrections expenditures to other state expenditures, it is possible to construct an initial story about how equilibration might operate in monetary terms. In this simple formulation, the growth rate of other state expenditures serves as the "engine" for the system. When this growth increases, for example, the growth of corrections expenditures increases. However, the positive relationship between the two growth rates does not allow for equilibration. Equilibration materializes through the log-ratio of the two variables, lagged by one year; the log-ratio serves as a "rudder" that keeps the growth rate of corrections expenditures on course.

It should be apparent now why, in the unrestricted form (equation 2), each of the terms are present at the lags indicted. For example, the error-correcting term cannot be specified at a lag of zero in equation 3b because, in the unrestricted form, the same variable would be on both sides of the equals sign. Similar comparisons between the restricted and unrestricted forms provide analogous arguments for the other terms. Equally important, the relationship between the restricted and unrestricted forms will be critical later when statistical tests for the equilibrating process are discussed.

If there is an equilibrating process, there should be some kind of stable outcome. In fact, there are two kinds. First, assume that the relationships represented in 3b are in "steady state." By "steady state" is meant that the original variables are growing at a constant *rate* (i.e., the growth rate is a constant). For example, the steady-state growth rate for corrections expenditures might be .05 (i.e., 5 percent per year). In other words, a steady state allows for change, but at a constant rate. (See BRMC for more discussion.)

Assuming a steady-state, one can return to equation 3b, insert the steady-state growth rates for the growth rate variables, and solve for the error correction term. This yields:[2]

$$\exp \left[-\frac{\delta_1}{\delta_3}(S)^* + \frac{1}{\delta_3}(C)^* \right] = \frac{C}{S} = \text{a constant} \qquad [4]$$

Where the "exp" indicates that we have taken antilogs, and the asterisks are used to represent the steady-state growth rates (which can be negative and are therefore perhaps better conceptualized as rates of change, not necessarily growth). These operations led BRMC to conclude that Blumstein's constant ratio of the number of people punished to the overall population could be understood as a steady-state outcome. Here, the point is similar; in steady state, there is a constant ratio (note that the ratio is not subscripted) of corrections expenditures to all other public expenditures. Put in other terms, while the log-ratio error correction term serves as a rudder keeping corrections expenditures on course, that course's destination is the steady-state balance between corrections expenditures and all other state expenditures.

Rephrased in terms used by BRMC, the steady-state ratio provides a target toward which the system aims. Note, however, that, since this target is a function of the two regression parameters and the two steady-state growth rates, different political jurisdictions might well have different steady-state constants. For example, societies experiencing a large influx of immigrants might invest more heavily in a sanctioning apparatus (relative to other public goods).

A second and more restrictive concept of stability can be defined through the total *absence* of growth (or change); all motion stops. Looking at equation 3b, since corrections expenditures at time t by definition now equal corrections expenditures at time t-1, the righthand side equals zero and the growth rate formulation becomes uninteresting; all change has ceased. However, returning to equation 2 and inserting constants (e.g., the means) representing the values at which the variables are frozen, the standard equilibrium solution follows for a bivariate difference equation:

$$\ln(\bar{C}) = \frac{(\delta_1 + \delta_2)}{(1 - \gamma)} (\bar{S}) \qquad [5]$$

If one has *substantive* reasons to capitalize on dynamic relationships frozen in time, static equilibrium solutions can be instructive. Perhaps the major use of static solutions such as those shown in equation 5 is represented in the concept of a "total multiplier" (Harvey, 1981: 291). A total multiplier is the total (asymptotic) change in an endogenous variable resulting from a specified change (usually a unit change) in a given regressor. We shall, however, make no use of total multipliers in this chapter.

An Initial Test of Monetized Equilibration

With some technical preliminaries behind us, we can now turn to an initial test of monetized equilibration. Basically, we will apply equations 3a and 3b, the unrestricted and restricted models we have emphasized so far. For the endogenous variable, we will use the year-by-year growth of corrections expenditures (both operating and capital costs, in constant, 1967 dollars) for the California state prison system from 1860 to 1970.

While the BRMC data begin in 1851, just after California became a state, the corrections system was operated under contract to private parties until 1860. Moreover, the first several years of expenditures data show unusual variability and produce a number of outliers in the original and growth rate forms.

For the exogenous variable, we will use the total yearly expenditures for the state of California (in constant, 1967 dollars) over the same interval, with corrections expenditures subtracted.[3] As stressed by BRMC, such measures are clearly limited to sanctions provided by the state criminal justice apparatus (e.g., county jails are ignored), but, unlike earlier work at the state level, all sanctions delivered through the state corrections system are included. That is, sanctions affecting corrections expenditures are represented (e.g., parole).

The formal test of the error-correcting mechanism was alluded to earlier. In essence, one simply compares the error sum of squares from the restricted and unrestricted equations. Since these models are nested (i.e., the restricted form is contained within the unrestricted form) and differ by a single restriction (implying a difference of but one degree of freedom), the test is, in principle, unambiguous; the standard F-ratio will suffice (Harvey, 1981: 159-175, 183-185). A statistically significant F-ratio indicates that the unrestricted model is superior (i.e., one obtains a better fit with the unrestricted specification) and that equilibration is rejected.[4]

Of course, in order to obtain an error sum of squares, regression parameters must be estimated. BRMC briefly discuss statistical issues, and a detailed justification for ordinary least squares can be found in Davidson et al. (1978) and Hendry and Mizon (1978). In particular, there seems to be a consensus among these econometricians that, by and large, serially correlated residuals should not be treated as a mere nuisance and then swept under the rug with generalized least squares (often based on an ARIMA "noise model" framework) or related procedures. Rather, serially correlated residuals should be at least initially taken to indicate specification error (e.g., Harvey, 1981: 148-159), remedied, in principle, by altering the systematic component of the equation(s) being estimated. We will proceed in that spirit here.

One can obtain a sense of the underlying patterns we hope to capture by looking at Figures 3.1, 3.2, and 3.3. In Figures 3.1 and 3.2 corrections expenditures and state expenditures (minus corrections expenditures) are plotted over time. In general terms, both show similar patterns of growth; both "take off" shortly after World War II. Moreover, the mean growth rate of corrections expenditures (i.e., .054) is close to the mean growth rate of state expenditures (i.e., .065). Yet, the ratio of the two is hardly constant. Figure 3.3 shows that even after disregarding some large fluctua-

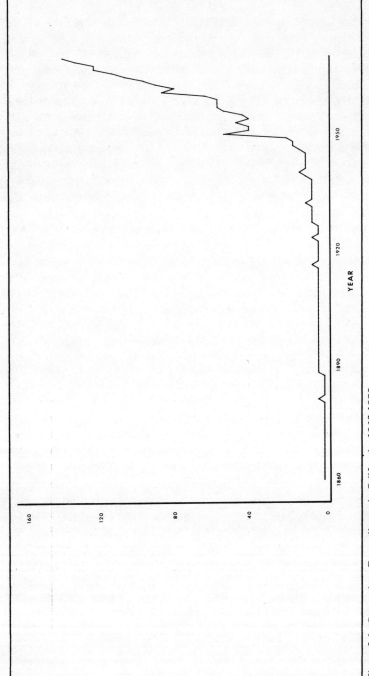

Figure 3.1 Corrections Expenditures in California, 1860-1970

NOTE: Expenditures are in millions of 1967 dollars.

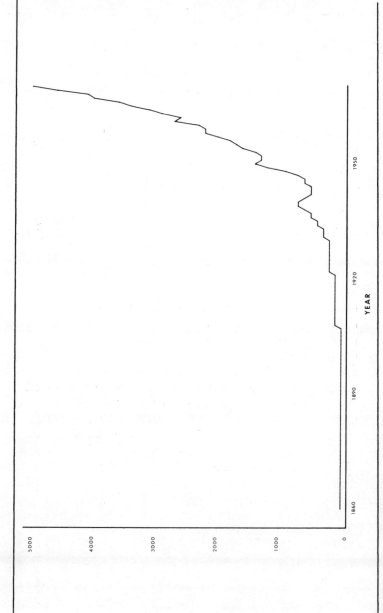

Figure 3.2 Other State Expenditures in California, 1860-1970

NOTE: Expenditures are in millions of 1967 dollars.

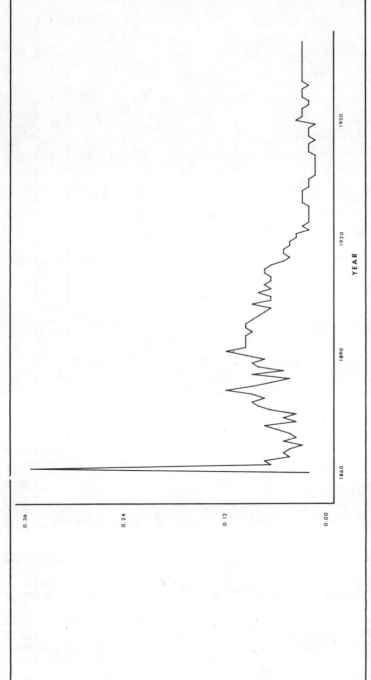

Figure 3.3   Ratio of Corrections to Other State Expenditures in California, 1860-1970

NOTE: Expenditures are in millions of 1967 dollars.

tions early in the series, corrections expenditures achieve their largest ratio to other state expenditures during the progressive era (i.e., the turn of the century), drop to a low level during the Great Depression, and then make a modest recovery after World War II. At first glance, such patterns seem systematic enough to raise doubts about the importance of a steady-state constant, but it is difficult to argue from Figure 3.3 alone. Our equilibrating model allows for random variation around the steady-state constant, through the inclusion of a disturbance term (see equation 3b).[5]

Table 3.1 permits us to be more precise. The top panel shows the results for the restricted equation, and the bottom panel shows the results for the unrestricted equation. It is important to stress that both equations passed the usual array of tests one applies when working with time series data. For example, although the autocorrelation and partial autocorrelation functions for the residuals from the restricted equation showed some evidence of serial correlation, adding a lagged value of the endogenous variable (i.e., to model the serial correlation) did not substantially alter the results. Further discussion on related statistical issues is provided by BRMC.[6]

From the top panel, there appears to be slight support for an equilibrating model. Both regression coefficients are in the predicted direction, and the t-value for the error correction mechanism is −2.39. Unfortunately, the lower panel indicates that the error sum of squares is cut substantially, and, as a result, the restricted model is rejected with an F-ratio of 8.93. Adding lagged values of the endogenous variable reduced the value of the F-ratio, but the restricted model was still unambiguously rejected. In short, we basically replicate the findings reported by BRMC; there is no evidence for an equilibrating process within the formal model implied by the traditional stability of punishment hypothesis. However, along with BRMC, we can raise the possibility of more complicated equilibrating processes, which, while outside of the traditional stability of punishment hypothesis, are still consistent with its spirit. We turn to such models now.

MODEL II:
A CORRECTING MECHANISM
WITH A SHIFTING TARGET

We noted earlier that while the stability of punishment hypothesis required approximately constant levels of punishment within a given society, different levels in different societies were allowed. But why limit such disparities to cross-sectional comparisons? Why not develop models that equilibrate, but equilibrate to different levels of punishment as

TABLE 3.1   A Test of Model I for the Growth Rate of California Corrections Expenditures, 1860-1970

Restricted Form:

$$\ln\left(\frac{C_t}{C_{t-1}}\right) = \alpha_1 \ln\left(\frac{C_{t-1}}{C_{t-2}}\right) + \alpha_2 \ln\left(\frac{S_t}{S_{t-1}}\right) +$$

$$\alpha_3 \ln\left(\frac{C_{t-1}}{S_{t-1}}\right) + \ln(a_t)$$

Variable		Coefficient	t-Value
α_1	Growth rate of corrections expenditures, t-1	-0.558	-7.21
α_2	Growth rate of state expenditures, t	0.144	0.54
α_3	Corrections expenditures/state expenditures, t-1	-0.027	-2.39

ESS = 12.141   df = 108 R^2 = .37

Unrestricted Form:

$$\ln\left(\frac{C_t}{C_{t-1}}\right) = \beta_1 \ln(C_{t-1}) + \beta_2 \ln(C_{t-2}) + \beta_3 \ln(S_t) +$$

$$\beta_4 \ln(S_{t-1}) + \ln(a_t)$$

Variable		Coefficient	t-Value
β_1	ln of corrections expenditures, t-1	-0.702	-8.12
β_2	ln of corrections expenditures, t-2	0.457	5.57
β_3	ln of state expenditures, t	0.210	0.81
β_4	ln of state expenditures, t-1	-0.003	-0.01

ESS = 11.205   df = 107 R^2 = .42

F test = 8.93 (1,107 df)
(for the reduction in ESS from the restricted to the unrestricted form)

historical circumstances change? Thus, during periods of economic crisis, there may be increased pressure to crank up the sanctioning apparatus. Conversely, participation in popular wars might reduce the need for punishment. It is important to emphasize that there can still be an error-correcting mechanism. However, the rudder steers a different course depending on the nature of the times. That is, the equilibrating process permits a discrete number of steady-state, target ratios.

In this spirit, consider the following equation:

$$\ln\left(\frac{C_t}{C_{t-1}}\right) = \lambda_1 \ln\left(\frac{S_t}{S_{t-1}}\right) + \lambda_2 \ln\left(\frac{C_{t-1}}{S_{t-1}}\right) + \lambda_3(D_t) + \ln(a_t) \qquad [6]$$

where we have done nothing more than add a new variable to equation 3b: a dummy variable coded 1 during economic depressions and 0 otherwise. If one accepts the arguments made by BRMC, the dummy variable's regression coefficient may well be positive. That is, during hard times, incarceration growth rates increase, which in turn may increase the growth rate of corrections expenditures. On the other hand, while BRMC do find that poor economic conditions increase incarceration growth rates, there may also be fewer tax dollars to support costly sanctions. Consequently, one might argue that the dummy variable has no effect, or perhaps even a negative effect. In any case, should the dummy variable prove important, the intercept in the equation (here assumed to be zero) will be shifted in a discrete manner. Note, however, that the equilibrating process described earlier remains intact, and the error-correcting mechanism is still in place. The steady state implications can be seen in equation 7.

$$\exp\left\{-\frac{\lambda_1}{\lambda_2}(\overset{*}{S}) + \frac{1}{\lambda_2}(\overset{*}{C}) - \frac{\lambda_3}{\lambda_2}(D_t)\right\} = \frac{C_{t-1}}{S_{t-1}} \qquad [7]$$

This equation looks much like 4; indeed the two are identical except for the terms associated with the depression dummy variable. Since the dummy variable is not a growth rate, it cannot have a steady-state rate of growth. Therefore, the steady state does not transform the dummy variable into a constant rate of change, and it follows that the steady-state constant is shifted in a discrete fashion when the dummy variable shifts from 1 to 0 and back again. We have indicated this time dependency by subscripting both the dummy variable and the steady-state constant. Thus, if the depression regression coefficient is positive, the target ratio of corrections expenditures to other state expenditures will, when times are hard, be set at a higher level. The target will return to its "normal" level when the economic crisis ends. (This is premised on a negative regression coefficient for the error correction term.)

The introduction of dummy variables into the equilibration framework has little impact on the empirical procedures described earlier. Indeed, one simply adds one or more dummy variables as needed and proceeds just as before. Only when the time comes for interpreting the results are new considerations introduced; one must tell a "story" for any changes in the equation's intercept (normally equal to zero) and the closely related changes in the steady-state constant.

A Test of Model II

Building on the models estimated by BRMC, Table 3.2 shows the results when a number of discrete regressors are added to the equations discussed earlier (see Table 3.1). In brief, ten dummy variables were added to represent the introduction of important corrections programs and practices. Corrections reforms included the introduction of probation, parole, indeterminate sentencing, and the like. One dummy variable each was added for periods of economic depression, the introduction of New Deal social programs, and periods of social unrest. "Social unrest" was coded 1, for example, during the repression of the labor movement shortly after the turn of the century (Bean, 1978) and during the 1960s, when blacks and students in California were making life difficult for civil authorities. BRMC provide additional details about the corrections reforms included (see also Berk et al., 1982), and, for reasons that will become apparent shortly, we need not dwell on them here.[7]

There are also some technical issues about how properly to use the data inductively to help determine the lag structure of the regressors and whether or not the regressors should be differenced. Here too, BRMC provide some commentary, although a far more thorough account can be found in Harvey (1981: 243-250, 279-292). Suffice to say that the specifications represented in Table 3.2 were subject to a variety of specification tests and diagnostics and, given the available data, are probably the best models possible within a monetized equilibrating framework.

There is really very little news in Table 3.2. Despite considerable experimentation with different lag structures (risking Type I error), there is no evidence that the additional dummy variables have any causal impact. Indeed, an F-test on the joint hypothesis that all of the discrete effects are zero cannot be rejected at conventional significance levels. And, as before, the F-test on the increment in the error sum of squares decisively rejects the restricted specification with an F-ratio of 8.71.

Several conclusions follow. First, even allowing for a more flexible equilibrating process based on a shifting, steady-state target, we can find no evidence of equilibration. Our earlier model monetized the traditional

TABLE 3.2   A Test of Model II for the Growth Rate of California Corrections Expenditures, 1860-1970

Restricted Form:

$$\ln\left(\frac{C_t}{C_{t-1}}\right) = \alpha_1\ln\left(\frac{C_{t-1}}{C_{t-2}}\right) + \alpha_2\ln\left(\frac{S_t}{S_{t-1}}\right) + \alpha_3\ln\left(\frac{C_{t-1}}{S_{t-1}}\right)+$$

$$\alpha_4(1-B)CDP_t + \alpha_5(1-B)CIW_t + \alpha_6(1-B)SS_t +$$

$$\alpha_7(1-B)CRC_t + \alpha_8(1-B)CYA_t + \alpha_9(1-B)D_t +$$

$$\alpha_{10}(1-B)ISL_t + \alpha_{11}(1-B)ND_t + \alpha_{12}(1-B)Pa_t +$$

$$\alpha_{13}(1-B)Pr_t + \alpha_{14}(1-B)PSA_t + \alpha_{15}(1-B)CU_t +$$

$$\alpha_{16}(1-B)WWII_t + \ln(a_t)$$

Variable		Coefficient	t-Value
α_1	Growth rate of corrections expenditures, $t-1$	-0.562	-6.87
α_2	Growth rate of state expenditures, t	0.105	0.36
α_3	Corrections expenditures/ state expenditures, $t-1$	-0.028	-2.26
α_4	County diagnostic program (binary)	0.074	0.21
α_5	California Institute for Women (binary)	-0.215	-0.60
α_6	Split-time sentencing (binary)	0.055	0.15
α_7	California Rehabilitation Center (binary)	0.269	0.76
α_8	California Youth Authority (binary)	-0.126	-0.35
α_9	Depression (binary)	-0.001	-0.01
α_{10}	Indeterminate sentencing (binary)	-0.187	-0.53
α_{11}	New Deal programs (binary)	0.027	0.09
α_{12}	Parole (binary)	-0.061	-0.17
α_{13}	Probation (binary)	0.070	0.20
α_{14}	Probation Subsidy Act (binary)	0.034	0.10
α_{15}	Civil unrest (binary)	-0.034	-0.30
α_{16}	WW II release program (binary)	-0.248	-0.85

ESS = 11.807   df = 95 R^2 = .39

(continued)

TABLE 3.2   Continued

Unrestricted Form:

$$\ln\left(\frac{C_t}{C_{t-1}}\right) = \beta_1\ln(C_{t-1}) \quad + \quad \beta_2\ln(C_{t-2}) \quad + \quad \beta_3\ln(S_t) \quad +$$

$$\beta_4\ln(S_{t-1}) \quad + \quad \beta_5(1-B)CDP_t \quad + \quad \beta_6(1-B)CIW_t \quad +$$

$$\beta_7(1-B)SS_t \quad + \quad \beta_8(1-B)CRC_t \quad + \quad \beta_9(1-B)CYA_t \quad +$$

$$\beta_{10}(1-B)D_t \quad + \quad \beta_{11}(1-B)ISL_t \quad + \quad \beta_{12}(1-B)ND_t \quad +$$

$$\beta_{13}(1-B)Pa_t \quad + \quad \beta_{14}(1-B)Pr_{t-} \quad + \quad \beta_{15}(1-B)PSA_t \quad +$$

$$\beta_{16}(1-B)CU_t \quad + \quad \beta_{17}(1-B)WWII_t \quad + \quad \ln(a_t)$$

Variable		Coefficient	t-Value
β_1	ln of corrections expenditures, t-1	-0.714	-7.81
β_2	ln of corrections expenditures, t-2	0.454	5.24
β_3	ln of state expenditures, t	0.179	0.64
β_4	ln of state expenditures, t-1	0.040	0.14
β_5	County Diagnostic Program (binary)	0.094	0.28
β_6	California Institute for Women (binary)	-0.260	-0.76
β_7	Split-time sentencing (binary)	-0.042	-0.12
β_8	California Rehabilitation Center (binary)	0.287	0.84
β_9	California Youth Authority (binary)	-0.232	-0.67
β_{10}	Depression (binary)	0.002	0.02
β_{11}	Indeterminate sentencing (binary)	-0.144	-0.42
β_{12}	New Deal programs (binary)	0.025	0.09
β_{13}	Parole (binary)	0.054	0.16
β_{14}	Probation (binary)	0.162	0.47
β_{15}	Probation Subsidy Act (binary)	0.106	0.31
β_{16}	Civil unrest (binary)	-0.002	-0.02
β_{17}	WW II release program (binary)	-0.240	-0.86

ESS = 10.805   df = 94 R^2 = .44

F test = 8.71 (1,94 df)
(for the reduction in ESS from the restricted to the unrestricted form)

stability of punishment hypopthesis and came up empty. Now, a generalization within the spirit of the Durkheim-Blumstein approach also fails.

Second, however, the results for the unrestricted model clearly indicate that the growth rate of corrections expenditures has important systematic variation that can be partly captured. While serious multicollinearity in the bottom equation prevents interpretation of any of the regression coefficients, there is no dispute that lagged values of the state and/or corrections expenditures are at least useful predictors; together they account for over 30 percent of the variance in the growth rate of corrections expenditures. In short, there is a story to be told, even if that story cannot be extracted from Table 3.2.

Third, there is no evidence that any of the dummy variables have important effects despite considerable fiddling with the lag structure (risking Type I error). While this parallels the findings for the policy variables examined by BRMC, there are special grounds for caution here. In particular, the unrestricted equation, while accounting for a meaningful portion of the variance, is almost certainly misspecified. (The restricted equation has already been rejected through the F-test.) Moreover, BRMC find important effects for measures of economic conditions, yet none surface here. Therefore, a reasonable conclusion is that there is systematic variation in the growth rate of corrections expenditures but that its causes remain a mystery. Perhaps under a more accurate specification policy effects would be found.

MODEL III:
A CORRECTING MECHANISM
WITH A MOVING TARGET

Suppose that, under Model II, we had found a large number of statistically significant effects for the policy dummy variables. This would have meant that the target ratio of corrections expenditures to all other state expenditures would have been shifting in a discrete fashion every few years. Suppose now that one carried this logic a step farther and allowed the steady-state target to shift in every time period. In effect, the log-ratio would move "continuously" in discrete time. There would no longer be anything approximating a stable, steady-state target for the equilibrating process, but *there would still be equilibration.* There would still be a rudder making midcourse corrections; however, in each time period, a new destination would be determined.

Equilibrating models allowing for a "continuously" moving target are easily developed and are often quite instructive. Consider equation 8:

$$\ln\left(\frac{C_t}{C_{t-1}}\right) = \psi_1 \ln\left(\frac{S_t}{S_{t-1}}\right) + \psi_2 \ln\left(\frac{C_{t-1}}{S_{t-1}}\right) +$$

$$\psi_3(D_t) + \psi_4 \ln\left(\frac{M_t}{M_{t-1}}\right) + \ln(a_t) \qquad [8]$$

Equation 8 is the same as 7, except that a new variable has been added. The equation now includes the growth rate for the size of the armed forces, measured by the rate of growth for the number of individuals in the service. If the arguments made by BRMC hold here, the regression coefficient associated with the military growth rate should be negative (other things being equal). At the very least, major wars take large numbers of young men out of circulation (as military recruits and, later, casualties). Since young men account for a large proportion of crimes, the crime rate, and then the rate of incarceration, should decline. Less growth in corrections expenditures may follow.

Perhaps more interesting is the role of the military growth rate when corrections expenditures and all other state expenditures are in steady-state. If one is prepared to define a steady state for the growth rate of military personnel, one is essentially returned to equation 4; there is a single, steady-state ratio, although its precise value is now a function of an additional parameter and an additional, steady-state growth rate. However, suppose that it is misleading to define a single steady state for the military growth rate. At a minimum, there may be two steady states: one during war and one during peace. The result is comparable to equation 7; there are now two steady-state ratios.

But this may still be unsatisfactory. Since World War II, there has been substantial variation in the size of the military (and its rate of growth) independent of formal hostilities. Moreover, the recent growth of the military in the absence of war (but in the service of readiness) indicates that the peacetime of today is quite different from the peacetime of earlier periods. In short, it may be hard to define a meaningful steady state.

The consequences for the steady-state ratio of corrections expenditures to overall state expenditures can be seen in equation 9.

$$\exp\left\{-\frac{\psi_1}{\psi_2}(\overset{*}{S}) + \frac{1}{\psi_2}(\overset{*}{C}) - \frac{\psi_3}{\psi_2}(D_t) - \frac{\psi_4}{\psi_2}\left(\frac{M_t}{M_{t-1}}\right)\right\} = \frac{C_{t-1}}{S_{t-1}} \qquad [9]$$

It is apparent that the military growth rate now plays a role in determining the steady-state target. However, since no steady state is defined for the military growth rate, it is free to vary from year to year. Thus, the steady-state target varies from year to year as well. It is important to stress that there is still a steady state for the other growth rates, and consequently one can speak about a steady-state target. However, that target can now change "continuously" in discrete time.

To summarize, the introduction into a dynamic equilibrating formulation of any noncategorical variable without a meaningful steady state allows the steady-state target to vary from period to period. This does not eliminate the "rudder" inherent in dynamic equilbrating relationships. However, it does permit the ship to change its destination in a continuous fashion. The critical question is when a regressor can possess a steady state. If the regressor is not defined in growth rate form, there is no ambiguity; without a growth rate, there can be no constant rate of growth. For example, had we included the logarithm of the military, instead of its growth rate, a continuously moving target would have resulted. In contrast, when the additional regressor is a growth rate, one's only recourse is theory and a grounded understanding of what the variable is meant to measure. Often, there will be no clear answers.

A Test of Model III

With Table 2.2 as a baseline, nothing of interest changes when the growth rate of the military and the growth rate of California prisons are introduced into both the restricted and unrestricted equations. Again, equilibration is rejected with a substantial F-ratio, and the new variables prove unimportant. And as before, while over 30 percent of the variance is explained under the unrestricted model, there is ample evidence of specification error. When this is combined with extremely high multicollineary, it is apparent that no substantive story can be extracted. In short, something is going on, but the causes remain unknown.

AN ALTERNATIVE DYNAMIC MODEL
OF CORRECTIONS EXPENDITURES

It seems fair to conclude that the monetized formulations we have tried show little promise. Our findings, therefore, parallel those of BRMC: We can find no evidence for equilibration for either the traditional or generalized stability of punishment perspective. However, this is not to say that if one is interested in the time path of corrections expenditures, instructive dynamic models cannot be found. And while space limitations here preclude a full examination of the possibilities, we offer one approach that possesses some genuine potential, based, as before, on rational polynomial functions.

To start simply, suppose that each year criminal justice officials (and especially corrections officials) seek some desired level of expenditures. That is, there is some amount of support to which they aspire and toward which they work. Suppose also that this desired level is a linear function of funding provided to all other state services. In particular:

$$DC_t = \beta(S_t) \qquad [10]$$

where DC_t is the desired level of support, S_t is the level of funding for all other state services, and β is some constant. In practice, β is likely to be a positive number and a fraction. For example, the ratio of desired expenditures for the corrections system to expenditures for all other state-funded services may be .05; in other words, for every \$100 provided for all other state services, criminal justice officals seek \$5 for support of the corrections system.

As a practical matter, however, the desired expenditures level cannot be immediately achieved. There are a host of obstacles, including competing claims on tax dollars, ineffective lobbying efforts, and political opposition to corrections goals (e.g., Berk et al., 1977). Consequently, one can define a "reaction function":

$$(C_t - C_{t-1}) = \gamma(DC_t - C_{t-1}) + a_t \qquad [11]$$

where C_t are actual corrections expenditures, γ is a coefficient that is larger than zero and no larger than 1.0, and a_t is a random disturbance. Equation 11 indicates that the greater the gap between actual corrections expenditures the previous year and current desired expenditures, the greater the difference between the previous year's expenditures and the current year's expenditures. For example, the reaction function implies that when, compared to the previous year, criminal justice officials feel there is lots of ground to be made up, the increment between the previous year's expenditures and expenditures obtained in the current year is likely to be especially large. There are, however, two caveats. First, if γ is small, the ground will not be made up rapidly, but will take several years. Second, a large disturbance can speed or slow the adjustment process.

Formulations such as these are called "partial adjustment" models and have been widely applied in economics (Kmenta, 1971: 476-477; Harvey, 1981: 226-227). Substituting equation 10 into equation 11, one obtains:

$$(C_t - C_{t-1}) = \gamma\beta(S_t) - \gamma(C_{t-1}) + a_t \qquad [12a]$$

or

$$C_t = \gamma\beta(S_t) + (1-\gamma)(C_{t-1}) + a_t \qquad [12b]$$

either of which may be estimated in a consistent fashion with linear ordinary least squares (Kmenta, 1971: 487), assuming white noise residuals. However, the linear results still require a bit of arithmetic to generate the values of all the desired coefficients and do not usually provide all of the significance tests needed. When the proper software is available, one is better off employing nonlinear ordinary least squares because significance tests for the coefficients of interest are routinely provided. In any case, we need to extend equation 10 (and, by implication, 12a and 12b) to include other factors that might affect desired expenditures:

(1) the number of offenders under custody and supervision;
(2) changes in corrections policy and practice, such as the introduction of parole and probation or the building of new prisons; and
(3) major historical events, such as economic crises, that might alter the opportunities and/or aspirations for funding corrections activities.

Within these three broad categories, there are, of course, a number of specific variables that might be considered. In the absence of any firm theoretical guidelines or compelling prior research, we proceeded initially by simply including all of the regressors used earlier. It was hardly inconceivable that each could affect the support level sought. In addition, we included as a regressor the total number of offenders under custody or supervision (excluding the number on probation). Finally, since we assumed that each regressor altered the desired *level* of expenditures in an *additive* manner (as in equation 10), neither logarithms nor first differences were employed.[8]

Unfortunately, when the full model was estimated in the appropriate (nongrowth rate) form, there was immediately evidence of serious multicollinearity. The largest condition index (Belsley et al., 1980: 96-117) was well in excess of 50, and there were two especially problematic variables: the counter for the number of prisons and the size of the military. The former was highly associated with the lagged value of corrections expenditures and the number of offenders in prison or on parole. The latter was linked to all variables increasing exponentially over time. At the risk of introducing specification errors, we dropped the prison counter and replaced the military variable with a dummy variable coded 1 in periods of war and 0 in periods of peace.

TABLE 3.3   Nonlinear Least Squares Results for a Partial Adjustments
Model of California Corrections Expenditures, 1860-1970

$$(C_t - C_{t-1}) = \gamma \sum_{k=1}^{16} \beta_k X_{tk} - \gamma C_{t-1} + a_t$$

Variable	Coefficient	t-Value
Corrections expenditures, t-1 (γ)	0.924	11.58*
All other state expenditures (β_1)	0.023	10.58*
	R^2 = .52	F = 60.63* (2,109 df)
Prison and parole population, t-1 (β_2)	612.125	2.71*
	R^2 = .52	F = 1.28 (1,108 df)
Policy and practice changes ($\beta_3 - \beta_{12}$)	--	--
	R^2 = .68	F = 6.11* (10,98 df)
Historical events ($\beta_{13} - \beta_{16}$)	--	--
	R^2 = .69	F = 2.38 (4,94 df)

*p<.05

There is not space here to consider the full set of results from the equation that followed, but the highlights are presented in Table 3.3. The variables are listed along the lefthand margin in order of theoretical importance: the basic partial adjustment variables, the number of offenders in prison or on parole, all changes in corrections policies and practices, and important historical events. When single variables are shown, we report the regression coefficient and associated t-value based on the full (unrestricted) model. For each cluster, where no single measure of causal effect makes sense, we present the incremental adjusted R^2 along with the F-test on that increment to variance explained. These provide a general sense of whether the cluster provides some explanatory power. The rationale for these packaging shortcuts will be apparent as we proceed.

The first two variables form the heart of our partial adjustment model. At the very least, we assume that desired expenditures depend on the level of funding provided to all other state functions (see equation 10). In addition, the adjustment process introduces a lagged value of corrections expenditures on the righthand side of the equation (see 11 and 12a). These two variables alone account for over 50 percent of the variation in differenced corrections expenditures. Equally important, the regression coefficients are statistically significant and make sense. The regression coefficient for lagged corrections expenditures is an estimate of the adjustment coefficient. Since the coefficient is near 1.0 (i.e., .92), the adjustment process operates (see equation 11) very rapidly. The regression coefficient for all other state expenditures is an estimate of the constant of proportionality between corrections expenditures and all other expenditures. From Table 3.3, it appears that the ratio of the two is about .025. In other words, for every $100 dollars of other state expenditures, about $2.50 goes to corrections. Note that this seems roughly consistent with Figure 3.3.[9]

Perhaps the next most important variable, from a theoretical viewpoint, is the number of offenders in prison or on parole. It stands to reason that corrections officials might establish desired levels of funding based on the number of people for whom they are held responsible. In fact, the number of people in prison or on parole lagged by one year (since this is the most recent figure likely to be available) shows some promise. When added to the model after the first two variables, little more variance is explained. However, the t-value from the full model is well over 2.0, and the regression coefficient indicates, for every additional person under supervision, the change score is incremented by $612.[10]

There is also some promise when the two clusters of variables are considered. Table 2.3 indicates that both contribute to the variance explained, although the F-ratio for historical events falls just short of statistical significance at the .05 level. In other words, it is probably safe to say that variables from both clusters affect desired expenditures. The problem is that multicollinearity among variables in these clusters precludes any compelling estimates of causal impacts. For example, the effective dates for the introduction of parole and probation are about a year apart, and the dummy variables for the two reforms correlate well over .90. Under these circumstances, it is very difficult to determine their independent effects. There is a story to be told, but it cannot be extracted with the current model.

To summarize briefly, if one is interested in explaining temporal patterns in corrections expenditures for the state of California, partial adjustment models may have a lot to offer. While formal statistical tests cannot be used to compare our earlier dynamic, error-correcting formulations with the partial adjustment approach (because the two specifications are not nested within one another and do not even share the same form of the endogenous variable), it is intriguing that while the error-correcting specifications explain an upper bound of 11 percent of the variance in the corrections expenditures growth rate, the partial adjustment specification explains an upper bound of about 70 percent of the variation in differenced corrections expenditures.

CONCLUSIONS

Our conclusions are rather straightforward. First, consistent with BRMC, we find no evidence for the traditional stability of punishment hypothesis when it is formulated in monetary terms. Second, and also consistent with BRMC, we find no evidence for more general statements of the stability of punishment perspective, again in monetary terms. This is not to say that other kinds of dynamic equilibrating processes cannot be at work. Indeed, in a related analysis based on a rather different theory, dynamic error-correcting mechanisms play a significant role (Berk et al., 1982). Finally, if one is interested in historical variation in corrections expenditures, partial adjustment models look promising. While we would hesitate putting much faith in the particular coefficients reported above, the overall results certainly support a partial adjustment approach.

NOTES

1. If the relationship is not stable, equilibration is beside the point. Thus, stability is a reasonable assumption.

2. In steady state, the disturbance is set to its expected value of zero.

3. Corrections and state expenditures for 1860 to 1910 come from Fankhauser (1913). Subsequent years are taken from biennial (1911 to 1948) and later annual (1949 to 1970) reports of the state controller. Both corrections and state expenditures from 1860 to 1950 are on a cash basis; expenditures in a given year are only those monies actually paid out and do not include bills received but not yet paid. Those expenditures are included in later years as they are paid out. Beginning with the 1951 fiscal year, California switched to a modified accrual system of reporting, where all bills received are included in each year's expenditures, but monies paid out to cover the cost of prior years are not. Unfortunately, information in the controller's reports after 1951 does not include the necessary data with which to separate actual expenditures from monies owed. Conversations with officials in the state controller's office made it clear that such information was available but would involve checking each state agency's records for each year since 1951. Consequently, expenditures from 1951 to 1970 are on a modified accrual basis.

4. This comparison assumes that one or the other model is the correct one. If both are misspecified, the test is inappropriate.

5. In the early years, the corrections system earned small amounts of revenue from the work of prisoners. These earnings are not included here because prison revenues do not reflect a cost borne by society. However, the amount of revenue is far too small to make much of a difference in any case.

6. The absence of an intercept in this and later models follows from the initial formulation discussed under equation 2. More concretely, an intercept would imply the existence of a *deterministic* trend in the time path for the log of corrections

expenditures (not in growth rate form). There is no theoretical reason for including such a trend. A detailed discussion of the role of "trend parameters" can be found in Box and Jenkins (1976: 92-93).

7. For readers without easy access to Berk et al. (1981), the policy changes include the effective introduction of probation, starting in 1906; the effective introduction of parole, starting in 1907; the effective change to indeterminate sentencing in 1919; the change to split-time sentencing, starting in 1928, which allowed judges to sentence convicted offenders to jail as a condition for probation; the opening of the California Institute for Women in 1932; the program during World War II allowing some prisoners to be released to work in war industries; the effective introduction of the California Youth Authority in 1945, which established a separate supervisory body for corrections facilities serving minors; the introduction of the County Diagnostic Program in 1957, which allowed for psychological assessments of convicted offenders before sentencing; the introduction of the Civil Addict Program in 1961, which established a separate treatment facility for addicts and "decriminalized" addiction; and the Probation Subsidy Act in 1965, which provided direct subsidies to counties employing probation as an alternative to incarceration.

8. It is worth noting in passing that the partial adjustment model is equilibrating, in the sense that when all variables affecting desired expenditures are taken as constants and the disturbance is set to its expected value of zero, a *static* equilibrium results. However, since no growth rates are involved, one cannot talk in a meaningful way about steady-state solutions or dynamic equilibria. It may also be worth noting that the intercept in the equation specifying desired expenditures is implicitly zero because, when all the regressors are set to zero, it means (among other things) that state expenditures for all other public services are zero. If a state is spending no money on such services, it is likely that there will be no money for corrections. Of course, since California became a state, a variety of state services have been funded.

9. The partial adjustment equation passed the usual array of time series diagnostics; the residuals were white noise.

10. We also estimated models adjusting for apparent heteroscedasticity. The results were virtually identical.

REFERENCES

BEAN, W. (1978) California: An Interpretive History. New York: McGraw-Hill.
BECKER, G. S. (1968) "Crime and punishment: an economic approach." J. of Pol. Economy 76: 169-217.
BELSLEY, D. A., E. KUH, and R. E. WELSCH (1980) Regression Diagnostics: Identifying Influential Data and Sources of Collinearity. New York: John Wiley.
BERK, R. A., H. BRACKMAN, and S. LESSER (1977) A Measure of Justice. New York: Academic Press.
BERK, R. A., D. RAUMA, and S. L. MESSINGER (1982) "Simultaneous macrodynamic models of incarceration rates: a comparison of historical patterns in California for male and female offenders." Unpublished manuscript, University of California, Santa Barbara.

——— and T. F. COOLEY (1981) "A test of the stability of punishment hypothesis: the case of California, 1851-1970." Amer. Soc. Rev. 46: 805-829.

BLUMSTEIN, A. and J. COHEN (1973) "A theory of the stability of punishment." J. of Criminal Law and Criminology 64: 198-207.

BLUMSTEIN, A. and S. MOITRA (1979) "An analysis of the time series of the imprisonment rates in the states of the United States." J. of Criminal Law and Criminology 70: 376-390.

BLUMSTEIN, A., J. COHEN, and D. NAGIN (1977) "The dynamics of a homeostatic punishment process." J. of Criminal Law and Criminology 67: 317-334.

BOX, G.E.P. and G. M. JENKINS (1976) Time Series Analysis: Forecasting and Control. San Francisco: Holden-Day.

CAHALAN, M. (1979) "Trends in incarceration in the United States since 1880." Crime and Delinquency 25: 9-41.

CHIANG, A. C. (1974) Fundamental Methods of Mathematical Economics. New York: McGraw-Hill.

DAVIDSON, J.E.H., D. F. HENDRY, F. SRBA, and S. YEO (1978) "Econometric modelling of the aggregate time-series relationship between consumers' expenditure and income in the United Kingdom." Economic J. 88: 661-692.

DURKHEIM, E. (1964a) The Division of Labor in Society. New York: Free Press.

——— (1964b) The Rules of Sociological Method. New York: Free Press.

FANKHAUSER, W. C. (1913) "A financial history of California, 1849-1910." University of California Publications in Economics, Vol. III.

GOLDBERG, S. (1958) Introduction to Difference Equations. New York: John Wiley.

GREENBERG, D. F. (1980) "Penal sanctions in Poland: a test of alternative models." Social Problems 28: 194-204.

——— (1977) Mathematical Criminology. New Brunswick, NJ: Rutgers Univ. Press.

HARVEY, A. C. (1981) The Econometric Analysis of Time Series. New York: John Wiley.

HENDRY, D. F. and G. E. MIZON (1978) "Serial correlation as a convenient simplification, not a nuisance: a comment on a study of the demand for money by the Bank of England." Economic J. 88: 549-563.

KMENTA, J. (1971) Elements of Econometrics. New York: Macmillan.

PERRY, M. E. (1980) Crime and Society in Early Modern Seville. Hanover: Univ. Press of New England.

RAUMA, D. (1981) "Crime and punishment reconsidered: some comments on Blumstein's stability of punishment hypothesis." J. of Criminal Law and Criminology 72: 1772-1798.

RUGGIERO, G. (1980) Violence in Early Renaissance Venice. New Brunswick, NJ: Rutgers Univ. Press.

STIGLER, G. J. (1970) "The optimum enforcement of laws." J. of Pol. Economy 78: 526-536.

THEIL, H. (1978) Introduction to Econometrics. Englewood Cliffs, NJ: Prentice-Hall.

VOTEY, H.L., Jr. and L. PHILLIPS (1973) "Social goals and appropriate policy for corrections: an economic appraisal." J. of Criminal Justice 1: 219-240.

WALLER, I. and J. CHAN (1974) "Prison use: a Canadian and international comparison." Canadian Law Q. 17: 47-71.

William F. Eddy
Stephen E. Fienberg
Diane L. Griffin
Carnegie-Mellon University

4

LONGITUDINAL MODELS, MISSING DATA, AND THE ESTIMATION OF VICTIMIZATION PREVALENCE

The National Crime Survey (NCS), designed and executed by the U.S. Bureau of the Census, produces national data on crime victimization in the United States on an ongoing basis. Based on a stratified, multistage cluster sampling plan, the NCS utilizes a rotating panel of household locations. We give further details of the sample design in section 1 (see also Fienberg 1978, 1980b). From its inception in 1972, the NCS has been used almost exclusively to produce incidence rates by type of crime and selected characteristics of the victims and/or offenders of the kind found in NCS annual reports (see U.S. Department of Justice, 1981b).

In March 1981, the Bureau of Justice Statistics (BJS), which sponsors the NCS, issued a report (U.S. Department of Justice, 1981a) on the prevalence of crime, in which the key quantity estimated was the percentage of households touched by crime in a given year. In this chapter we describe some stochastic longitudinal models for victimization that can be used to produce such an annual prevalence rate, and we show how the BJSs reported prevalence measure relates to those we have derived. More-

AUTHORS' NOTE: This material is based in part on work performed under Contract No. J-LEAA-015-79 with the Bureau of Justice Statistics, and in part on subsequent work performed under Grant 81-IJ—CX-0087 from the National Institute of Justice, both in the Office of Justice Assistance Research and Statistics, U.S. Department of Justice. Points of view and opinions stated herein are those of the authors and do not necessarily represent the official position or policies of the U.S. Department of Justice.

over, following a suggestion of Albert Biderman, we adopt a cheery approach to the otherwise depressing prevalence measure by taking its complement—the percentage of crime-free households in a given year.

For purposes of this study we need to distinguish among the housing unit (HU) or location, the household (HH) or family living in that unit, and the individuals who compose the household. As we note in section 1, at each interview NCS respondents provide victimization information on the preceding six months. To actually determine whether an HU (or an HH) has been "touched by crime" it is, in principle, necessary to examine all of the interviews of the occupants of the HU (or members of the HH) that contain information for some part of the year in question. Typically this will mean that we need information from a respondent for three successive interviews to reconstruct the victimization profile for a single year, and that the data will need to be matched or linked in some type of longitudinal format.

In practice, we do not get to see a complete longitudinal record for each housing unit, household, or individual for any specific twelve-month period of interest. When an HU enters or leaves the sample during the year, part of the desired data will be missing. Similarly, data for six-month intervals can be missing for individuals or households (HH) due to non-interviews. Finally, if the NCS is viewed as an HH sample rather than an HU sample, then missing data can occur as a result of households and individuals who move between interviews. Any attempt to construct prevalence indicators of crime must directly address the problems of missing data and their relationship to the data that are not missing. We give some clues as to the dimensions of the missing data problem for our prevalence measures in section 3, linking actual missing data rates to officially published nonresponse rates.

From a methodological research perspective our interest would normally focus on the development of stochastic models for longitudinal victimization records (see, e.g., the discussion in Fienberg 1978, 1980b), and such a perspective remains a critical feature of the cheery indicator problem. Some simplifications ensue when we restrict our attention to prevalence measures, however, and these allow us to make progress on a modeling problem that would otherwise appear to be virtually intractable. For example, longitudinal modeling typically would require a time-ordered victimization history, but, as Reiss (1980) and Fienberg (1980b) note, NCS data have ordering problems when series victimizations or multiple victimizations occur. From a prevalence perspective, these ordering problems do not really matter—all we need to know is that at least one victimization (perhaps of a given type) has occurred. Such simplifications, when combined with the interest in prevalence measures by the Bureau of Justice Statistics, has guided our methodological efforts.

In this chapter we develop several "naive" stochastic longitudinal models in which missing data are assumed to be missing at random. Fragmentary evidence available from analyses by Reiss and others suggests little support for such an assumption, and efforts to model "missingness" will be part of our future activities. We refer to the models described here as naive because each is based on a large number of inappropriate but simplifying assumptions, and because they reflect little of the structure described in longitudinal analyses by Reiss (1980) and by Fienberg (1980a, 1980b), for example. Moreover, we fit the models in section 5 only to data on HUs, not to longitudinal files on HHs or on individuals, and we treat victimizations in an aggregate form, not distinguishing among types. We present these naive models and results from their preliminary application to establish a starting point for future modeling and analysis efforts that we hope will incorporate more appropriate and substantively interesting assumptions.

1. NCS SAMPLE DESIGN

In this section we give a brief synopsis of the rotating panel design of the NCS, because this structure is so critical to an understanding of the NCS longitudinal data base discussed in section 2. For further details see Fienberg (1980b) and U.S. Department of Justice (1980, 1981b).

The NCS is based on a stratified, multistage cluster sample. The first stage consists of dividing the United States into 1,931 primary sampling units (PSUs) comprising counties or groups of continguous counties. The PSUs are then separated into 376 strata, 156 of which are self-representing. From the remaining 220 strata one PSU is selected from each stratum with probability proportional to population size. Within each of the 376 PSUs selected, a systematically chosen group of enumeration districts is selected, and then clusters of approximately four HUs each are chosen within each enumeration district. This method produces a self-weighting probability sample of dwelling units and group quarters within each chosen PSU. For 1979, this process led to the designation of about 62,000 HUs, and interviews were obtained from occupants of about 51,000. Most of the remaining designated HUs were vacant or otherwise deemed ineligible for inclusion in the NCS; about 2,200 of these HUs would actually be labeled nonrespondents.

The basic sample is divided into six subsamples or rotation groups of about 9,000 HUs each. The rotation groups are numbered 1 through 6 within each sample. Every six months a new rotation group enters the sample and the "oldest" existing rotation group from the previous sample is dropped. Each rotation group is divided into six panels with panel 1 being interviewed in January and July, panel 2 in February and August,

TABLE 4.1   Rotation Scheme*

	Rotation Group											
	Sample A						Sample B					
Month	1	2	3	4	5	6	1	2	3	4	5	6
Jan.	1	1	1	1	1	1	1					
Feb.	2	2	2	2	2	2	2					
Mar.	3	3	3	3	3	3	3					
Apr.	4	4	4	4	4	4	4					
May	5	5	5	5	5	5	5					
June	6	6	6	6	6	6	6					
July		1	1	1	1	1	1	1				
Aug.		2	2	2	2	2	2	2				
Sept.		3	3	3	3	3	3	3				
Oct.		4	4	4	4	4	4	4				
Nov.		5	5	5	5	5	5	5				
Dec.		6	6	6	6	6	6	6				
Jan.			1	1	1	1	1	1	1			
Feb.			2	2	2	2	2	2	2			
Mar.			3	3	3	3	3	3	3			
Apr.			4	4	4	4	4	4	4			
				•								
				•								
				•								

*Numerical entries represent panel numbers within samples.

and so on. This process spreads the workload of the field staff. Each HU is in the survey for three full years for a total of seven interviews. (There are, however, some HUs that, due to the initial implementation of the rotation schedule, actually had as many as eight or nine interviews.) The data collected at the first of the seven interviews are used for bounding purposes—that is, to establish a time frame intended to avoid duplication of victimization information in subsequent interviews. These data are not incorporated into the official BJS reported rates (either incidence or prevalence) but have been incorporated into rates reported in this chapter.

Table 4.1 shows the rotation scheme. For instance, in September, panel 3 in each of the rotation groups 2 through 6 of sample A and 1 and 2 of sample B will be interviewed. In the following March, panel 3 of rotation group 2 in sample A is replaced by panel 3 of rotation group 3 in sample B.

At each interview information is acquired on the "household" as well as on all persons age 12 or older living in the designated HU. The interview questionnaires are used to record information about the household and the persons comprising it, as well as details on victimization events occurring during the previous six months. There is no guarantee of continuity of households or persons in the sample. If a household moves and is replaced by a new one, the experiences of the new household and its members are recorded at the time of the next interview. If the household composition changes, only information on those persons who are currently members is recorded. As a consequence, despite the fact that the entire rotation group of housing units provides "bounding information" at each interview, there is no bounding information available for a large proportion of households and especially persons for any given interview.

NCS data are aggregated on a quarterly basis to produce quarterly estimates of the volume and rates of victimization. Annual estimates are produced by pooling quarterly estimates. Care must be taken to distinguish *collection* months (i.e., the month in which data are collected) from *reference* months (the month to which the data relate). Data are actually stored by collection quarter (three months), each of which contains data for 8 reference months. Conversely, sample data from 8 collection months are required to produce estimates for each reference quarter. For a full reference year, data from 17 collection months are used, involving 8 rotation groups and 47 panels. More detailed discussions of the relation between reference and collection months may be found in Fienberg (1980b) and Penick and Owens (1976).

The NCS questionnaire distinguishes between individual identifiable incidents and series of at least three similar incidents which the respondent is unable to separate in time and place of occurrence. Either may be personal or household victimizations. For individual victimizations, the questionnaire records the month in which the crime took place. For series victimizations, the method of recording involves the details for only the most recent event in the series and the date of *first* occurrence. Prior to 1979, the respondents were asked to indicate the number of incidents (3-4, 5-10, 11+) and the quarter(s) in which the incidents took place: winter (December to February), spring (March to May), summer (June to August), and fall (September to November). In January 1979 this procedure was altered, and now respondents provide the number of incidents (not necessarily using the earlier grouping), and a breakdown of this count into quarters of the year (January-March, April-June, July-September, and October-December), rather than simple indicators for seasons.

In this chapter we include series victimizations, but we treat them as having occurred only in the first month in which the series occurred. This use of series victimizations reflects the way in which the data were coded for 1972-1976, the time frame of our longitudinal files, and not how they should be used as a consequence of the more detailed reporting scheme initiated in 1979. The estimates clearly lead to underestimates of the extent of victimization.

2. NCS DATA BASE

The NCS victimization data are publicly available through the Inter-University Consortium for Political and Social Research (ICPSR) at the University of Michigan. These data are grouped into quarterly collection files which include records of all the interviews completed by the U.S. Bureau of the Census for a particular three-month period. Because the occupants of a specific housing unit are interviewed every six months, each quarterly collection file contains the records for at most one interview for that housing unit.

Three types of information are collected by the NCS: Household Items, Individual Items, and Crime Incident Reports. Because households have varying numbers of individuals and individuals report varying numbers of crime incidents, it is not sensible to think of these data (nor is it feasible to store them) in a rectangular array with each row representing a housing unit, household, or even individual. ICPSR stores the data in an OSIRIS IV hierarchical file. OSIRIS IV is a proprietary software package developed and maintained at the Survey Research Center at the University of Michigan. It is a sequential file which can also be interpreted as a three-level hierarchy: household (H), person (P), and incident (C). The sequential order of the data records collected at one interview for two particular households, the individuals within those households, and the crime incidents reported by those individuals might be as follows:

Household record for HU #1
Person record for P #1 in HU #1
Incident record for C #1 for P #1 in HU #1
Person record for P #2 in HU #1
Incident record for C #1 for P #2 in HU #1
Incident record for C #2 for P #2 in HU #1
Person record for P #3 in HU #1
Household record for HU #2
Person record for P #1 in HU #2
Person record for P #2 in HU #2
Incident record for C #1 for P #2 in HU #2

The first household has three individuals; the first individual reported one crime incident and the second individual reported two crime incidents. The second household has two individuals; the second individual reported one crime incident.

Six months later (two collection quarters) these two housing units might be eligible for another interview. In that case the relevant quarterly OSIRIS file would contain similar data records for the two housing units.

Of course, the exact pattern might be different, as the occupants of the housing unit may change and the reported incidents, if any, will be different. It has been convenient for the analyses, which we describe below, for us to have these data reorganized into longitudinal files with all of the data for one housing unit together in chronological order, rather than scattered over many quarterly collection files. While we have not yet completed this reorganization directly from the ICPSR tapes, we were fortunate to obtain, from Professor Albert Reiss of Yale University, longitudinal files covering the period July 1, 1972 to December 31, 1976. These longitudinal data are divided into three separate files: The first contains only the household records; the second contains only the person records; and the third contains only the crime incident records. Each one of the three files can be regarded as a rectangular array with each row being, respectively, a household interview record, a person interview record, or a crime incident report.

The structure of the three longitudinal files for the same two particular housing units described above is as follows, assuming the first housing unit was interviewed for the third time and the second housing unit was interviewed for the first time during the collection quarter indicated above. The information from above is indicated by italics.

Household File

Household records for HU #1 at first 2 interviews
Household record for HU #1 (Third interview)
Household records for HU #1 at subsequent interviews
Household record for HU #2 (First Interview)
Household records for HU #2 at subsequent interviews

Person File

Person records for P #1 in HU #1 at first 2 interviews
Person record for P #1 in HU #1 (Third Interview)
Person records for P #1 in HU #1 at subsequent interviews
Person records for P #2 in HU #1 at first 2 interviews
Person record for P #2 in HU #1 (Third Interview)
Person records for P #2 in HU #1 at subsequent interviews
Person records for P #3 in HU #1 at first 2 interviews
Person record for P #3 in HU #1 (Third Interview)
Person records for P #3 in HU #1 at subsequent interviews
Person record for P #1 in HU #2 (First Interview)
Person records for P #1 in HU #2 at subsequent interviews
Person record for P #2 in HU #2 (First Interview)
Person records for P #2 in HU #2 at subsequent interviews

Incident File

Incident records for P #1 in HU #1 at first 2 interviews
Incident record for C #1 for P #1 in HU #1 (Third Interview)
Incident records for P #1 in HU #1 at subsequent interviews
Incident records for P #2 in HU #1 at first 2 interviews
Incident record for C #1 for P #2 in HU #1 (Third Interview)
Incident records for P #2 in HU #1 at subsequent interviews
Incident records for P #3 in HU #1 at first 2 interviews
Incident records for P #3 in HU #1 - None at Third Interview
Incident records for P #3 in HU #1 at subsequent interviews
Incident records for P #1 in HU #2 - None at First Interview
Incident records for P #1 in HU #2 at subsequent interviews
Incident record for C #1 for P #2 in HU #2 (First Interview)
Incident records for P #2 in HU #2 at subsequent interviews

In the Household File there is one record for each interview. Thus, the lines not in italics in this example represent data records. In the Person File and the Incident File there are records only when data are actually collected. As a consequence, the lines not in italics in this example may or may not represent actual data records. This example does not reflect the full complexity of the Person File and the Incident File because the individuals within a household may vary from interview to interview and because the household itself (within the housing unit) may change from interview to interview. We have ignored this additional complexity in the analyses described below by focusing on housing units and not on households.

Data for the housing units in each of the three files are stored in the same order with respect to an internal identification number. This makes cross-references among the three files fairly simple. Although the data can still be thought of in the household-person-incident hierarchy, it is simpler to conceptualize questions and execute programs on rectangular files. When more than one level of the hierarchy is involved in an analysis, special programming will be required (just as with the OSIRIS IV hierarchical files), but since each of the three files is rectangular, the job will be simpler.

For the purposes of this study we have chosen to work not with the full longitudinal data base, but rather with a systematic random sample of 1,539 household locations (every one-hundredth HU). As a consequence we need not address ourselves to the current controversy regarding the use of sample weights in model-based statistical analyses (for some discussion of this matter see Fienberg, 1980b). Virtually all clustering effects are removed as a result of the systematic sampling, and the estimates described in section 4 are derived for simple random sampling (i.e., ignoring the NCS sample design). All of the results reported in section 5 are computed from this sample of 1,539 HUs and thus are subject to substantially greater variability than those estimates that we ultimately plan to compute for the full NCS data base.

3. MISSING DATA AND WEIGHTED ANALYSES

One of the most troublesome aspects of longitudinal modeling for sample survey data is the handling of missing data. In a cross-sectional analysis aggregate quantities are typically estimated by applying assigned weights to sample units. As an example, in the NCS for personal crimes these weights are the product of a "basic weight" times a "within-household noninterview factor" times a "duplication control" times a "household noninterview factor" times a "first-stage ratio-estimate factor" times a "second-stage ratio-estimate factor." The two "noninterview factors" are adjustments for missing data that are computed, within appropriate subgroups, as the ratio of the count of possible interviews to the count of actual interviews.

For cross-sectional analysis missing data involving full records for a given month is a problem of limited magnitude. For longitudinal analyses it remains to determine the magnitude of the missing data problem. To this end we counted, for each of the 1,539 HUs in our sample, the number of months of missing data. Because of the fact that interviews cover six-month periods, Table 4.2 is organized with six months in each row. For example, the entry in row 2 and column 3 gives the number of HUs with $(6 \times 2)+3 = 15$ missing months. We note that all 1,539 HUs are included in Table 4.2 regardless of the length of time between July 1972 and December 1976 that they were listed as housing units participating in the survey. For instance, some of the HUs in the (0,0) cell were in the survey for only 1 interview, while some were in the survey for eight. Moreover, a household with only one interview may contribute as little as one month to the reference period of interest.

In our sample of 1,539 HUs, only 916, or about 60 percent, have complete records for that part of the July 1972 to December 1976 period. According to the most recent NCS report (U.S. Department of Justice 1981b), 96 percent of all eligible HUs participated in the survey. On the average, an HU from our 1 percent sample for 1972-1976 was in the survey for 4.25 interviews. Thus, if we assume that missing interviews occur independently of one another, we would expect roughly $(0.96)^{4.25}$ or about 84 percent of our HUs to have complete records for the July 1972 to December 1976 period. The 96 percent nonresponse figure is not really applicable here, however.

BJS reports that for 1979, of the approximately 62,000 HUs sampled, interviews were obtained from the occupants of about 51,000. Of the

TABLE 4.2   Number of Housing Units in Sample with 6K + I
Months of Missing Data

K \ I	0	1	2	3	4	5
0	916	8	7	10	15	5
1	229	5	3	3	2	5
2	100	2	3	1	4	2
3	65	1	5	1	1	1
4	49	2	5	4	0	2
5	25	1	0	2	3	2
6	17	3	2	1	0	1
7	12	2	0	0	0	3
8	6	1	0	0	0	2

remaining 11,000 HUs, about 2,200 were occupied by persons who were not interviewed because they could not be reached, and about 8,800 were found to be vacant, demolished, converted to nonresidential use, or otherwise ineligible. The 96 percent figure is the percentage of HUs deemed eligible that responded—that is, 51,000/(51,000+2,200) = 96%. Table 4.2 included *all* sampled HUs, and thus the appropriate response figure is 51,000/62,000 or about 82 percent. Thus, if we assume, as before, that missing interviews occur independently of one another, we would expect roughly $(.82)^{4.25}$ or 43 percent of the HUs in the 1 percent sample to have complete records, substantially less than the observed 60 percent.

The U.S. Bureau of the Census (n.d.) reports that about 2 percent of the processed HUs are units that had no address listed on the listing sheet, had been demolished, had moved (i.e., trailer), had been converted to a business, or had merged with another unit. Removing these units from the 62,000 sampled units yields a response rate of about 84 percent. With this response rate, assuming again that missing interviews occur independently of one another, we would expect roughly 48 percent of the HUs in the 1 percent sample to have complete records. The fact that about 60 percent of the 1,539 HUs have complete records suggests that the missing interviews may not occur independently of each other and that missingness may be positively correlated over time.

Even if the proportion of records with missing data were not as great as that indicated by Table 4.2, we believe that it still would not be advisable to construct weighted aggregates using the weights described at the beginning of this section, and to do "weighted analyses" of the longitudinal data base. This is simply because the weights change from interview to interview. It is tempting to argue that the weights should not change much and one could use an "average" weight. Such is not the case. Several households in our sample exhibited substantial variation in the sample-based weights. For example, in one selected unit, the household weight varied from 964.996 to 1120.389, while the weight for one of the persons in the household varied from 874.662 to 1389.469. We believe that a more thoughtful model-based approach, rather than the blind application of sample-based weights, is required to take into account the implication of the sample design on statistical analysis (see the related discussion in Fienberg, 1980b).

4. MODELS FOR VICTIMIZATION PREVALENCE MEASURES

The analysis of data sets from which some items are missing is often performed by ignoring the missing components. Such an analysis will lead to appropriate inferences only if the nonresponse mechanism does not depend on the values of the missing items. In particular, the missing data may be ignored if the assumption is made that whether or not an HU responds at a particular interview does not depend on whether or not that HU was victimized in the six months prior to that interview. When this condition holds, we will say that the missing data are missing at random (Little, 1980; Rubin, 1976). Although the validity of the "missing at random" condition cannot be checked directly, some preliminary analyses show that HUs with high proportions of missing data tend to exhibit higher rates of victimization than HUs with low proportions of missing data. The full impact of the "missing at random" assumption still needs to be assessed.

The remainder of this section is devoted to the exposition of several estimators of the percentage of crime-free HUs, θ. Some of these estimators are based on specific models of victimization and the "missing at random" assumption and others are more ad hoc in nature.

Estimator 1: An Ad Hoc Approach

We begin by considering an ad hoc estimator of the proportion of HUs not victimized by crime in a year:

(1) Consider each HU that had an interview covering at least one month of the year.
(2) If there is no victimization reported as having occurred in the year, consider the HU as being crime-free.

(3) For each HU determine the number of interview months in the year (that is, the number of months covered by an interview).

(4) Use as an estimator

$$\hat{\theta}_1 = \frac{\text{number of interview months for crime-free HUs}}{\text{total number of interview months}}. \qquad [1]$$

If an HU has reported a victimization in any month of the given year, then we are sure that it was not crime-free. With this in mind we may prefer a variation of θ_1:

$$\hat{\theta}'_1 = \frac{\text{CFM}}{12 \times \text{number of victimized HUs} + \text{CFM}} \qquad [2]$$

where CFM is the number of interview months for crime-free HUs (that is, the numerator of $\hat{\theta}_1$). Note that $\hat{\theta}'_1 \leqslant \hat{\theta}_1$.

Both $\hat{\theta}_1$ and $\hat{\theta}'_1$ have built-in biases that we expect will lead them to be overestimates (perhaps by a substantial amount) of some true proportion, θ. We note that they are, at least in spirit, similar to estimators, such as the Kaplan-Meier estimator, that appear in the survival analysis literature (e.g., see Kalbfleisch and Prentice, 1980).

Estimator 2: The BJS Estimator

Alexander (1981) describes two different estimators which were used to produce the prevalence rates published by the BJS (U.S. Department of Justice, 1981a). Because BJS needed to estimate rates for 1980 before the end of March 1981, and because it would be necessary to have information from interviews through June 1981 in order to calculate 1980 rates, BJS used information from 1980 interviews in place of information from interviews that would have occurred after January 1981. Thus, the BJS estimators used only two interview records rather than the three we require to obtain the information for an HU for a full calendar year. For example, BJS used the March 1980 and September 1980 interviews for an HU in panel 3, although the information obtained at these interviews is actually for the year September 1979 through August 1980 (see section 1).

In Appendix A we present a detailed description of the BJS estimates. Both are of a form similar to $\hat{\theta}_1$, except for the following:

(a) the time periods for interviews contributing to a given annual estimate extend backwards out of the period of interest,

(b) different weights are applied to different types of noninterviews, and
(c) $1-\theta$—that is, the probability of being victimized in a year—is estimated rather than θ.

In both cases the denominator of the estimator is interpretable as the number of interview months (divided by 12). For the first estimator, $\dot{R}_2$, the numerator consists of (a) the number of interviews obtained at HUs that completed all possible interviews and were also victimized at least once, plus (b) the number of interviews obtained at HUs for which one of the two interviews was missing and which also reported at least one victimization times a correction factor. This correction factor is used to adjust for the fact that HUs for which an interview is missing may or may not have been victimized during the months covered by the missing interview.

The second estimator, $\hat{R}'_2$, is similar to $\hat{R}_2$ except that the HUs that are missing the first interview and were victimized at least once are multiplied by a different correction factor than the HUs that are missing the second interview and were victimized at least once.

We note that the Bureau of Justice Statistics actually calculated these rates using the weighted counts referred to in section 3, while we have calculated them using the unweighted counts. In addition, we have used data from unbounded interviews and series as well as individual victimizations. For comparative purposes we compute $\hat{\theta}'_2 = 1-\hat{R}_2$ and $\hat{\theta}_2^2 = 1-\hat{R}'_2$ to estimate the proportion of crime-free HUs.

Estimator 3: Homogeneous Bernoulli Model

Estimator 3 is based on a homogeneous Bernoulli model of victimization. Let

$$x_{ij} = \begin{cases} 1 & \text{if HU } i \text{ is victimized at least once in month } j \\ 0 & \text{otherwise} \end{cases}$$

for $i = 1, \ldots, H; j = 1, \ldots, 12$, where H is the total number of HUs in the sample, be independent Bernoulli random variables with a common value of $p = \Pr\{x_{ij}=1\}$.

Under this model, every HU has the same probability, p, of being victimized in any month. A given HU is victimized in month j independently of whether or not it is victimized in month $\ell(\ell \neq j)$, and HU i is victimized independently of HU k $(k \neq i)$.

If we assume that the missing data are missing at random, it is easily shown (see Eddy et al., 1981) that the maximum likelihood estimator of p is

$$\hat{p} = \frac{V}{T} , \tag{3}$$

where T is the total number of x_{ij}'s that are observed and V is the sum of the observed x_{ij}'s—that is, V is the total number of months observed in which a victimization occurred.

If we wish to estimate θ, the probability that an HU is crime-free for the year, then we need only note that

$$\theta = (1-p)^{12} , \tag{4}$$

and thus the maximum likelihood estimator of θ is

$$\hat{\theta}_3 = (1-p)^{12} = \left(\frac{T-V}{T} \right)^{12}$$

$$= \left(\frac{\text{\# of crime-free months observed}}{T} \right)^{12} \tag{5}$$

Estimator 4: A Correlated Bernoulli Model

Tallis (1962) discusses a model that is a "mixture" or weighted average of the model of independence of victimizations across months described above and the model of perfect correlation in which an HU that is victimized in January is victimized every month and an HU that is not victimized in January is never victimized. In this model p represents, as above, the probability that an HU is victimized at least once in a given month. A second parameter, ρ $(0 \leqslant \rho \leqslant 1)$, represents the correlation between any two months of data for a given HU. In particular, letting x_{ij} be defined as above, we suppose that $(x_{i1}, \ldots, x_{i12})$, $i = 1, \ldots, H$, following the Tallis model and that $(x_{i1}, \ldots, x_{i12})$ is independent of $(x_{k1}, \ldots, x_{k12})$ for $i \neq k$.

As with the homogeneous Bernoulli model, every HU has the same probability p of being victimized in any month, and HU i is victimized independently of HU $k(k \neq i)$. This model has the feature that, when $0 < \rho \leqslant 1$, x_{ij} is no longer independent of $x_{i\ell}$ but when $\rho = 0$, this model simplifies to the Bernoulli model with complete independence of monthly observations.

Assuming that the missing data are missing at random, we can calculate the likelihood function in terms of p and ρ (details are given in Eddy et al., 1981). Unfortunately, this function cannot be maximized directly, and iterative methods are required to obtain maximum likelihood estimates of p and ρ. Two views of this likelihood are shown in Appendix B. Once we compute these estimates, it is then straightforward to compute the maximum likelihood estimate of θ, the proportion of crime-free HUs:

$$\hat{\theta}_4 = (1-\hat{\rho})(1-\hat{p})^{12} + \hat{\rho}(1-\hat{p})$$ [6]

Note that $\hat{\theta}_4$ is a linear combination of $\hat{\theta}_3$, the Bernoulli estimator, and $(1-\hat{p})$, the estimator that results from perfect correlation.

Estimator 5: A Markov Model

Let $x_{i1}, \ldots, x_{i12}$ be defined as above. We can consider these observations as arising from a two-state Markov chain with states 0 and 1, where 0 indicates that no victimization occurred within the month and 1 indicates that at least one victimization occurred. Let (p_0, p_1) be the initial probability vector, e.g., p_0 is the probability of no victimization in the initial month, and

$$\begin{pmatrix} p_{00} & p_{01} \\ p_{10} & p_{11} \end{pmatrix}$$ [7]

the transition matrix, e.g., p_{00} is the probability of no victimization in month i+1 *given* no victimization in month i. In addition, we assume that HU j is victimized independently of HU k and that the missing data are missing at random. As in the previous model, we are unable to maximize the corresponding likelihood explicitly, but iterative methods can be used to obtain maximum likelihood estimates of p_0, p_{00}, and p_{10}—that is, $\hat{p}_0$, $\hat{p}_{00}$, and $\hat{p}_{10}$. Several plots of the likelihood function are shown in Appendix B. The maximum likelihood estimate of θ, the proportion of crime-free housing units, is then

$$\hat{\theta}_5 = \hat{p}_0 (\hat{p}_{00})^{11} .$$ [8]

Note that $\hat{\theta}_5$ represents the probability of starting in the crime-free state in January and moving from the crime-free state to the crime-free state for each of the eleven successive months.

TABLE 4.3   Estimated Proportions of Households Untouched by
Crime, 1973–1975

	1973	1974	1975
Upper Bound	.753	.760	.770
$\hat{\theta}_1'$	.706	.719	.732
$\hat{\theta}_1'$	.676	.672	.695
$\hat{\theta}_2'$	.672	.689	.689
$\hat{\theta}_2'$	.671	.687	.687
$\hat{\theta}_3'$	.580	.583	.626
$\hat{\theta}_4'$	.626	.619	.651
$\hat{\theta}_5'$	.606	.613	.660
Lower Bound	.497	.519	.523

5. EMPIRICAL RESULTS: PRELIMINARY ESTIMATES
FOR VICTIMIZATION PREVALENCE

Using the sample of 1,539 household locations described in section 2, we have calculated values for the seven estimators presented in section 4. In addition, by assuming that every nonresponse month was a month in which a victimization occurred, we can compute a lower bound for $\hat{\theta}_1$. Similarly, by assuming that every nonresponse month was a crime-free month, we can calculate an upper bound for $\hat{\theta}_1$. While these bounds are strictly applicable to only $\hat{\theta}_1$, they are quite informative and suggest the range of possible estimates of $\hat{\theta}$ that can result from changes in model assumptions and specifications. In Table 4.3 we display the seven estimates and the bounds for the three years for which complete longitudinal data are available, 1973-1975. The estimated standard errors for several of these estimates are available, but are not reported here.

We note that $\hat{\theta}_1$, $\hat{\theta}_2$, $\hat{\theta}'_2$, $\hat{\theta}_3$, and $\hat{\theta}_5$ show a small increase from 1973 to 1974 and increase or remain the same from 1974 to 1975. On the other hand, $\hat{\theta}'_1$ and $\hat{\theta}_4$ decrease slightly from 1973 to 1974 and then increase from 1974 to 1975. All the changes are of relatively small magnitude. That is, the proportion of crime-free HUs seems to remain fairly constant over the 1973-1975 period.

In addition, we note that the "upper bounds" are relatively close to the values of $\hat{\theta}_1$, which we believe to be an overestimate of θ. The "lower bounds" lie far from $\hat{\theta}_3$, primarily because they treat a situation with a low value of p (the probability of victimization in a given month) as having occurred everytime we have missing data (something that happens quite often). Nonetheless, what we can learn from Table 4.3 is a rough range for θ (somewhere between 0.5 and 0.8).

6. EXTENSIONS AND PROBLEMS FOR FURTHER STUDY

This chapter has described some initial attempts to develop models for the analysis of longitudinal files constructed from a rotating sample survey. Our focus has been on the implications of such modeling for aggregate cross-section-like quantities—in this instance annual victimization prevalence rates for household locations (HUs). We do not believe that modeling NCS data longitudinally at the HU level makes very much sense. Thus the empirical results we report in section 5 are intended for illustrative purposes only. Even so, the estimates of the prevalence-related parameter θ reported there are clearly overestimates. This is because an HU can report information for a given six-month period in the NCS, but individuals within that HU can be nonrespondents and we have no information about their possible victimization experiences.

What should be clear from this discussion is that the missing data present a far greater problem for rotating panel surveys than has been acknowledged by those who conduct them. Indeed, reports of "monthly nonresponse rates" of 4-5 percent for the NCS give no clue to the magnitude of the missing problem that awaits the survey analyst who approaches survey data files organized longitudinally.

In section 4 we modeled the missing data as if they were missing at random. In fact, we believe that missingness may well be related to victimization experiences, and thus attention needs to be given to modeling missingness and victimization simultaneously.

Finally, we recall that we were able to act as if we had a simple random sample of HUs, even though such an assumption was inappropriate for the full longitudinal data file. Future modeling efforts will need to consider how the sample design characteristics should be reflected in the modeling and analysis process.

APPENDIX A: THE BJS ESTIMATORS

In order to describe the BJS estimators, Alexander (1981) presents a classification of each HU into one of six groups according to the number of interviews and the types of noninterview. There are three types of noninterview. A type A noninterview occurs when household members are rarely at home, uncooperative, or otherwise impossible to reach. A type B noninterview occurs when an HU selected for sample turns out to be vacant or otherwise ineligible. A type C noninterview occurs when an HU is found to be demolished, converted to nonresidential use, or otherwise out of the scope of the NCS. The six groups are as follows:

Group a: Both records are interviews.

Group b: Only the first record is an interview; the second record is missing because the HU was rotated out of the sample, or the second interview is a type A noninterview.

Group c: Only the second record is an interview; the first record is missing because the HU has just been rotated into the sample, or the first record is a type A noninterview.

Group d: The first record is an inverview; the second record is a type B or C noninterview.

Group e: The first record is a type B or C noninterview; the second is an interview.

Group f: Neither record is an interview.

From these groups, the following quantities are computed:

$H1 = $ # of HUs in group a.

$H4 = 1/2$(# of HUs in group b).

$H5 = 1/2$(# of HUs in group c).

$H6 = 1/2$(# of HUs in group d).

$H7 = 1/2$(# of HUs in group e).

$C1 = $ # of HUs in group a that report at least one victimization in either interview.

$C2 = 1/2$(# of HUs in group a that report at least one victimization in the first interview).

$C3 = 1/2$(# of HUs in group a that report at least one victimization in the second interview).

$C4 = $ same as C2 but for group b.

$C5 = $ same as C3 but for group c.

$C6 = $ same as C4 but for group d.

$C7 = $ same as C5 but for group e.

The BJS victimization prevalence rates are then given by:

$$\hat{R}_2 = \frac{C1 + C6 + C7 + (C4+C5)\,[C1/(C2+C3)]}{H1 + H4 + H5 + H6 + H7}$$

and

$$\hat{R}'_2 = \frac{C1 + C6 + C7 + C4[C1/2C2] + C5[C1/2C3]}{H1 + H4 + H5 + H6 + H7}$$

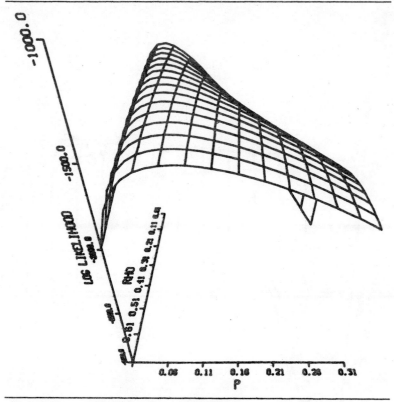

Figure 4.1   Log-Likelihood for 1973 Data with Series

APPENDIX B: LIKELIHOOD PLOTS

In order to obtain a more complete understanding of the maximum likelihood estimates, presented in section 4, for the correlated Bernoulli model and the Markov model, we have generated several graphs of the likelihood surface of each of these two models.

Figures 4.1 and 4.2 show two perspectives of the log-likelihood surface for the correlated Bernoulli model for the 1973 data. We can see that the surface has a unique maximum and so the maximum likelihood estimates are unique. Near the maximum the surface is much more peaked with respect to the variable p than with respect to ρ. In fact, from Figure 4.2, we note that near the maximum likelihood estimate of p, the surface is very nearly flat with respect to $\hat{\rho}$. Thus the variance of $\hat{\rho}$ is large compared to the variance of p. The log-likelihood surfaces for 1974 and 1975 data are similar to the one for 1973, as illustrated by Figures 4.1 and 4.2.

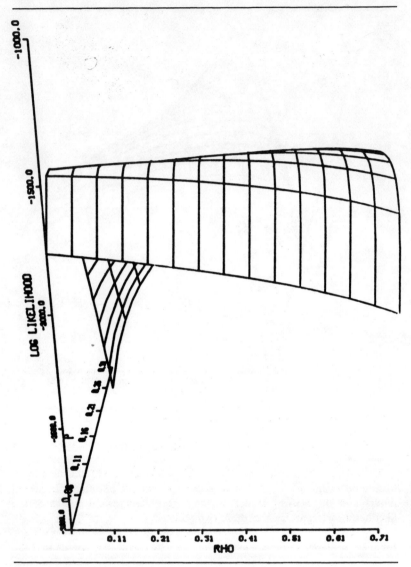

Figure 4.2   Log-Likelihood for 1973 Data with Series

Figures 4.3 to 4.7 are views of the likelihood surface for the Markov model with one parameter set equal to its maximum likelihood estimate. These five figures were generated using the 1975 data.

In Figures 4.3 and 4.4 p_0, the probability of initially being in the state 0 (nonvictimized), is set to the value of $\dot{p} = .954$. This log-likelihood

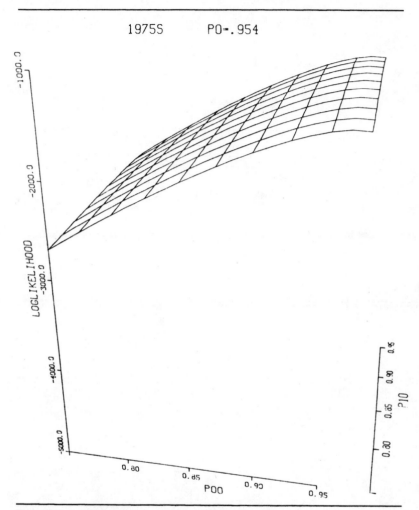

Figure 4.3 Log-Likelihood for Markov Model

surface is curved with respect to p_{00} much more than with respect to p_{10}, and so the variance of $\hat{p}_{00}$ will be small relative to the variance of $\hat{p}_{10}$. This is as we would have expected, since we have many more observations in the state 0 than in the state 1, and hence have more information about 0 to 0 transitions than about 1 to 0 transitions. Although it is not readily seen from these two figures, the maximum is unique.

Figures 4.5 and 4.6 show the log-likelihood surface with p_{10}, the probability of moving from state 1 to state 0, fixed at its maximum likelihood value of .838. We see that the surface is more curved in the p_{00} direction than in the p_0 direction. This is, again, what we would have

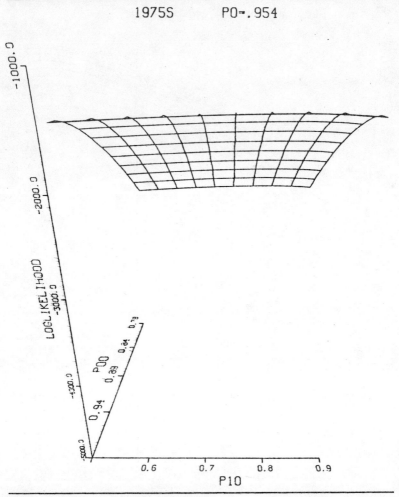

Figure 4.4 Log-Likelihood for Markov Model

expected, since there are many more 0 to 0 transitions than initial observations of the state 0. In these two figures it is possible by close inspection to see that the maximum is unique.

In Figure 4.7 p_{00}, the probability of moving from state 0 to state 0, is fixed to be .967. We see that this loglikelihood surface is extremely flat. Thus the variances of $\hat{p}_0$ and $\hat{p}_{10}$ will be relatively large and the values of $\hat{p}_0$ and $\hat{p}_{10}$ may not be very informative. It is vaguely discernible that a unique maximum occurs in the upper righthand portion of the figure.

The log-likelihood surfaces for the Markov model using data from 1973 and 1974 have characteristics similar to those displayed in Figures 4.3-4.7.

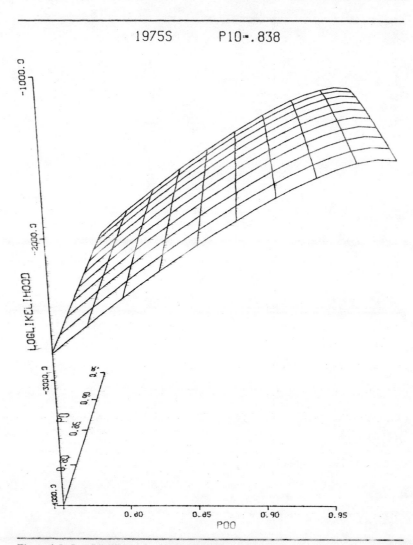

Figure 4.5 Log-Likelihood for Markov Model

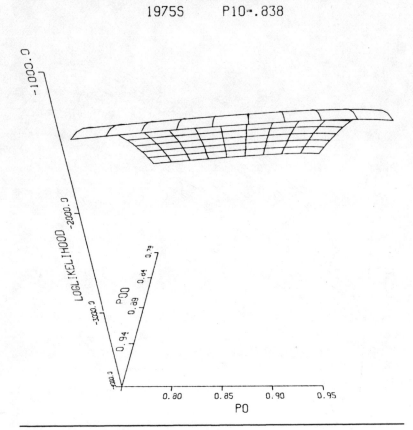

Figure 4.6   Log-Likelihood for Markov Model

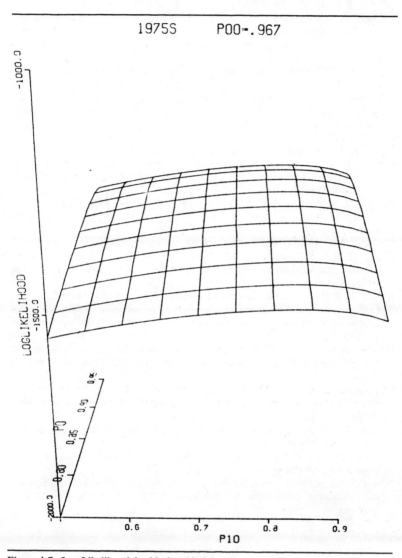

Figure 4.7 Log-Likelihood for Markov Model

REFERENCES

ALEXANDER, C. H. (1981) "Plans to produce National Crime Survey estimates of 'residences touched by crime.' " Unpublished Census Bureau memorandum.

EDDY, W. F., S. E. FIENBERG, and D. L. GRIFFIN (1981) "Estimating victimization prevalence in a rotating panel survey." Bulletin of the International Statistical Institute.

FIENBERG, S. E. (1980a) "Statistical modelling in the analysis of repeat victimization," pp. 54-58 in S. E. Fienberg and A. Reiss, Jr. (eds.) Indicators of Crime and Criminal Justice: Quantitative Studies. Washington, DC: Government Printing Office.

——— (1980b) "The measurement of crime victimization: prospects for panel analysis of a panel survey." The Statistician 29: 313-350.

——— (1978) "Victimization and the National Crime Survey: problems of design and analysis," pp. 89-106 in N. K. Namboodiri (ed.) Survey Sampling and Measurement. New York: Academic Press.

KALBFLEISCH, J. D. and R. L. PRENTICE (1980) The Statistical Analysis of Failure Time Data. New York: John Wiley.

LITTLE, R. (1980) "Superpopulation models for non-response II: the non-ignorable case." National Academy of Sciences, Committee on National Statistics Panel on Incomplete Data.

PENICK, B. K. and M.E.B. OWENS [eds] (1976) Surveying Crime. Report of Panel for the Evaluation of Crime Surveys. Washington, DC: National Academy of Science.

REISS, A. J., Jr. (1980) "Victim proneness by type of crime in repeat victimization," pp. 41-53 in S. E. Fienberg and A. Reiss, Jr. (eds.) Indicators of Crime and Criminal Justice: Quantitative Studies. Washington, DC: Government Printing Office.

RUBIN, D. B. (1976) "Inference and missing data." Biometrika 63: 581-592.

TALLIS, G. M. (1962) "The use of a generalized multinomial distribution in the estimation of correlation in discrete data." J. of the Royal Statistical Society B. 24: 530-534.

U.S. Department of Commerce, Bureau of the Census (n.d.) National Crime Survey, National Sample, Survey Documentation. Washington, DC: Government Printing Office.

U.S. Department of Justice, Bureau of Justice Statistics (1981a) "The prevalence of crime." Bureau of Justice Statistics Bull. Washington, DC: Government Printing Office.

——— (1981b) Criminal Victimization in the United States, 1979. Washington, DC: Government Printing Office.

——— (1980) Criminal Victimization in the United States, 1978. Washington, DC: Government Printing Office.

——— (1981c) National Crime Surveys: National Sample, 1973-1979. Ann Arbor: Inter-University Consortium for Political and Social Research, University of Michigan.

Marjorie S. Zatz

Arizona State University

5

DYNAMIC MODELING OF
CRIMINAL PROCESSING HISTORIES

Implicit in our conception of the criminal justice system is the notion that it is processual. Formal processing of defendants begins with arrest and continues through termination of parole, though defendants may leave the process at any of several decision points in between, and decisions reached at early stages influence later decisions. Nevertheless, processing models are rare in criminological research. The lack of such models does not appear to be the result of unawareness of the processual nature of criminal justice, since several researchers (e.g., Hagan, 1974; Burke and Turk, 1975; LaFree, 1980) have called for data and methodological techniques which focus on the defendant's experience in transit through the criminal justice process. More likely it reflects a paucity of such data and methodological techniques. Once criminal processing histories of defendants and the appropriate techniques for analyzing these data are available, formal models of criminal justice processing can be developed and tested. In so doing, the impacts of both exogenous factors and of prior outcomes on decisions at each stage of the criminal justice system can be assessed.

Given the existence of longitudinal data which constitute individual histories of criminal justice processing, methodological techniques which allow us to model the criminal justice system are required. Such tech-

AUTHOR'S NOTE: An earlier version of this chapter was presented at the annual meetings of the American Society of Criminology, Washington, D.C., November 1981. I would like to thank Peter J. Burke, Diane H. Felmlee, and Alan J. Lizotte for their helpful comments and suggestions, and Jordan L. Henderson and Karl Lehenbauer for assistance in data preparation. The data utilized in this study were collected and made available by the State of California Department of Justice, Bureau of Criminal Statistics. The Department of Justice bears no responsibility for the analyses or interpretations presented here.

niques must be able to take into account the variety of discrete outcomes, or destination states, which exist at each decision point. For example, the decision to sentence a defendant to a term of incarceration is both qualitatively different from and related to the decision to sentence a defendant to probation. Accordingly, a model is needed which will mirror the dynamic nature of criminal justice processing, handle the interrelations of discrete outcome states, and assess the effects of multiple exogenous factors.

The objective of this chapter is to provide an illustrative application of one such model, suitable for the study of the processing of individual defendants in continuous-time. It is argued here that use of such data and models can assist us in answering existing questions concerning criminal justice processing (e.g., whether or not members of different racial/ethnic groups are disposed of by the criminal justice system in different ways) and suggest new questions to be explored (e.g., whether or not the criminal justice processing time for members of different racial/ethnic groups differs and, if so, how this affects current and later outcome decisions). Furthermore, use of longitudinal data consisting of processing histories forces us to reconsider our notions of certain key concepts (e.g., recidivism) and foists on us reconceptualizations of these constructs. Thus, for example, the effects of recidivism are frequently included in cross-sectional studies through inclusion of "prior record" as an exogenous variable. Recidivism as a concept, however, acquires meaning only when we examine the initial and later types of criminal behavior in which individuals engage (if the concern is with criminal behavior per se) or the initial and later processings of individuals (if the concern is with criminal justice processing). Through use of longitudinal data and an appropriate methodological technique for analyzing such data, a reconceptualization of recidivism is suggested, along with a potentially fruitful method for investigating the effects of recidivism on criminal justice outcomes.

This study models the rate of transition from arrest to the point of case disposition to illustrate the use of a promising model for criminological research. The disposition points considered here are police release, prosecution denial of complaint, and (lower or superior) court. The point at which the case will reach disposition is the first decision faced by the organizations which comprise the criminal justice system following the arrest of an individual for a felonious offense. It concerns the agency ultimately responsible for disposing of the case, not the type of disposition. Accordingly, whether the type of disposition by court is plea or trial is of little consequence here, since that decision is made *after* the decision as to where to terminate the case.

The model chosen is one of a class of multivariate, finite-state, continuous-time, stochastic models described in detail by Tuma et al.[1] Maximum-likelihood estimates of the instantaneous rates of transition between categorical states are obtained through use of the program "RATE" (Tuma and Crockford, 1976). A transition between categorical states (i.e., an "event") is the unit of analysis, with the dependent variable consisting of an unobserved instantaneous rate of transition between the states. This rate is modeled as a function of exogenous variables.

As used here, the model is an extension of the simple Markov model involving modifications of the population homogeneity and time-stationarity assumptions. Advantages of the model over other methods of temporal analysis (e.g., panel data) include its full utilization of data, explicit inclusion of attrition as a categorical state, insensitivity to sampling and measurement error with moderate-sized samples (as shown in Tuma and Hannan, 1978), and its ability to predict the time path of several interdependent outcomes. In so doing, a variety of data-analytic procedures are parsimoniously unified into one model. Thus, for example, the probability of being in any of the three outcome states (police release, prosecution denial of complaint, or court case) at any point in time; the expected number of case dispositions by the police, prosecutor, and court in any given time interval; and the probability of leaving the origin state of arrest (and, thereby, moving into one or another of the disposition states) all constitute outcomes which can be predicted as functions of other, exogenous, variables by use of the RATE model. In addition, the effects of exogenous factors such as racial/ethnic membership on these outcomes can be assessed, and comparisons can be made among racial/ethnic groups through use of separate analyses for each group. It is possible, then, to trace the *actual* movement of individuals from one stage of the criminal justice system to the next, with explicit consideration of the interrelatedness of potential outcomes in processing decisions, over a period of time.

This method also leads to the reconceptualization of several traditional criminological concepts. For example, recidivists and nonrecidivists have typically been treated as two distinct groups, although the recidivist group has been further broken down into chronic and nonchronic recidivists (e.g., Wolfgang et al., 1972). Examination of longitudinal data consisting of individual criminal processing histories, however, leads us to the realization that *everyone* is a recidivist, but some persons have very low transition rates—that is, they take so long that they never come to the attention of social control agents. Dynamic models of criminal justice processing can ascertain these rates, as well as the probability of moving into one of several outcome states (such as being released by the police or being released by the prosecutor or going to court) in a given period of time. Thus, someone who is incarcerated for a long time, because he or she is incapacitated, requires a lengthy period before he or she can once again be arrested. Time-at-risk, then, is one aspect of rates of transition, and persons who have been incarcerated for a long time of necessity will have slower rates of transition than will persons released from incarceration more quickly or not incarcerated in the first place.

The traditional comparisons between the criminal behavior of recidivists and nonrecidivists or between the criminal justice processing of recidivists and nonrecidivists assume that recidivists and nonrecidivists form two distinct groups.[2] No such assumption is made here. Rather, this chapter addresses the question of whether or not the initial and later processings of the *same* individuals differ, whether as a consequence of knowledge of the criminal justice system accrued through earlier experiences with it, of increased visibility to the organizations which comprise the criminal justice system, or some other reason. Thus, what is of interest is how the effects of exogenous variables on the rates of transition between stages of the criminal justice system vary across processings of the *same* individual.

To address this question, the manner in which causal relationships (e.g., the effects of race/ethnicity on criminal justice processing) change over time must be ascertained. Furthermore, the impact of prior processing must be assessed. That is, the question arises as to whether any causal relationship found to exist between race/ethnicity and rates of transition from arrest to disposition for the first processing of individuals differs from that of second and later processing. If, for example, members of one racial/ethnic group are processed more quickly than are members of other groups, or reenter the criminal justice system faster than do others, then this very swiftness will affect their rates of transition.

In an attempt to answer questions such as these, the effects of exogenous factors, including duration in a state, on rates of transition to the three disposition points are examined for the first, second, third, fourth, fifth, and sixth or later "shifts," where a shift refers to an event, or the movement of a case from the origin state (arrest) to one of the destination states (police, prosecutor, or court). More specifically, the cases in the first shift include all persons who are arrested, regardless of whether they later reenter the criminal justice system and of their point of disposition. Similarly, cases in the second shift consist of all persons who have been arrested at least twice during the period of data collection, regardless of whether they reenter the criminal justice system for a third or later time and, once again, whatever the destination state (i.e., point of disposition). As such considerations demonstrate, questions concerning the manner in which causal relations change over time arise only when dynamic analyses of longitudinal data are undertaken. This is so because cross-sectional analytic techniques, which assume that the system under study has reached equilibrium, treat recidivism as a status rather than an aspect of criminal justice processing itself.

This reconceptualization of recidivism is of even greater import if it sheds light on the processing of members of different status groups, such as social class or race/ethnicity. Thus, Wolfgang et al. (1972) find a strong relationship between race (White, non-white) and recidivism in their examination of delinquency in a birth cohort. They focus attention primarily on the etiology of delinquency and on the characteristics of persons designated delinquent, using police contacts as a measure of recidivism. Such an approach assumes the validity of police reports.

One of the most problematic aspects of this assumption is the necessary belief that police contacts do not themselves vary by characteristics of the person (e.g., race/ethnicity, social class, sex, age) or by familiarity of the police with certain persons as a result of prior contacts. The conflict framework's focus on the criminal justice processing of members of different groups does not require such an assumption. In fact, it calls into question this very belief, making it a variable to be studied. Following this framework, it appears to be more reasonable to focus on differences among groups in their criminal justice processing shifts. In so doing, the effects of prior processings are controlled for and the impact of racial/ethnic membership on rates of transition to various outcomes can be ascertained for each processing of an individual.

Since the criminological literature has for some time been concerned with how race/ethnicity influences criminal sanctioning, primary focus is placed here on examining the effect of racial/ethnic membership (White, Black, Chicano) on rates of transition from arrest to disposition, both controlling for and in interaction with other legal and extralegal factors. The existing literature concerning racial/ethnic differences suggests little more than an assertion that for some offenses, in some jurisdictions, controlling for some legal and extralegal factors, at some stages of the criminal justice process, and using some methodologies, some groups are differentially treated. We have even less knowledge of the potential differential treatment of Hispanics, as compared with Whites and Blacks, largely as a result of the substantial lack of data on Hispanic offenders. The rapid growth of the Hispanic population in the United States and in the criminal justice system (Moore et al., 1978; Brewer, 1979; Sissons, 1979; Carro, 1980), then, makes explicit consideration of this group in criminal justice research critical.

An examination of rates of transition from one stage of the criminal justice system to the next for Whites, Blacks, and Chicanos should indicate whether differential treatment by race/ethnicity exists and, if it does, its manifestations. Use of the RATE model allows for a focus on the direct effects of racial/ethnic membership on these changes of state. It also allows for investigation of potential differences *between* racial/ethnic groups in the effects of exogenous factors on rates (through the comparison of separate analyses for each race/ethnicity) and differences *within* groups in the ways in which exogenous factors affect the rates of transition for each group.

More specifically, the illustrative analyses presented here focus on comparisons of the effects of exogenous factors on rates of change from arrest to each of the three destination states (police, prosecution, and court) for Whites, Blacks, and Chicanos and for all racial/ethnic groups combined. The results of these analyses for the first shift (regardless of whether or not the defendant returns to the criminal justice system in later shifts) and for sixth or later shifts are presented. Additionally, the effects of being Black and Chicano (both with reference to being White) on the transition rates to each disposition point are assessed for each of the first through sixth (or later)shifts to determine whether racial/ethnic membership affects these rates differently for different shifts. It should be noted here that the data base employed does not include any measure of social class. Therefore, effects of race/ethnicity could partly reflect class effects. Following the conflict framework, such class effects are to be expected. Nevertheless, differences in the processing of Blacks and Chicanos would imply the existence of race/ethnicity effects *beyond* those of class.

DESCRIPTION OF THE DATA

In order to examine criminal justice *processing,* suitable data which trace the actual transitions between stages of the criminal justice system are needed. The appropriate data must trace these transitions for individuals over a sufficiently long period to enable analysis of first, second, third, and later shifts.[3] Detailed event histories of criminal justice processing suitable for such analyses are, however, scarce. Thus, the first step in this study was to develop such a data set, reflecting the criminal justice processing histories of individuals.

The data were obtained from the State of California, Department of Justice, Bureau of Criminal Statistics. State of California data have been chosen because California is one of the few jurisdictions which codes race/ethnicity such that Hispanic defendants are readily identifiable. The data base consists of processing histories for persons whose cases were disposed of during the years 1977, 1978, and 1979, regardless of both the year of arrest and the type of disposition.[4] All arrests were for felony offenses.

The data include information on a variety of variables of interest for each offender, including demographic information, prior record of commitment, arrest and conviction offenses, and variables reflecting the processing of the case through the criminal justice system. The independent variables used to estimate rates of transition here include the defendant's race/ethnicity, sex, age,[5] arrest offense,[6] arrest offense severity,[7] and indicators of evidence[8] against the defendant. (See Tables 5.1 and 5.2 for categorizations of these variables.) Importantly, for each criminal case,[9] information exists on the date of arrest and on the date of disposition. Such dates are essential for a complete history of criminal processing and are used by the RATE program in estimating rates of transition. The original data set also included personal identifiers which, along with the arrest dates, allow for the extraction of first, second, third, and later processings of the same individual within a given time frame. For this illustrative analysis, the data consist of random samples of first, second, third, fourth, fifth, and sixth or later shifts for individuals.

PROCEDURES

A major problem which has plagued prior research on criminal justice sanctioning in general, and studies of differential sanctioning by social class or racial/ethnic membership in particular, has been the failure of our methodological techniques to deal adequately with processing. The conception of criminal justice as a process is not new, but the majority of prior studies have used cross-sectional data and analytic techniques, thereby making an implicit assumption that the system is at equilibrium. The dynamic model employed here makes no such assumption. In fact, it tests for time-dependence in the parameter estimates. Moreover, the model finds the unconditional probability of being in any specified state (including attrition) at any point in time.

The dependent variable is an instantaneous rate of transition from one qualitative state to another—in this case, from arrest to case disposition. This rate is roughly equivalent to transition probabilities in discrete time. It is defined as:

$$r_{jk}(t) = \lim_{\Delta t \to 0} \frac{P_{jk}(t, t + \Delta t)}{\Delta t}, \quad j \neq k \qquad [1]$$

where $P_{jk}(t, t + \Delta t)$ is the probability of a change from state j at time t to state k at time $t + \Delta t$. The instantaneous rate of transition $r_{jk}(t)$ is the limit, as Δt approaches zero, of the probability $P_{jk}(t, t + \Delta t)$, per unit of time.

This model is an extension of the simple Markov model, with modifications of the population homogeneity and time-stationarity assumptions.[10] According to the assumption of population homogeneity, the behavior of units under study (e.g., individuals) is governed by the same, constant

(text continued on page 104)

TABLE 5.1   Antilogs of Estimated Effects for First Shift to Each Destination State

Variables	All Race/Ethnicities	Whites	Chicanos	Blacks
Number of events:	10892	5496	2264	3132
		A. Police Release		
% of all events:	10.5%	8.7%	11.9%	12.6%
(Constant)	0.034*	0.032*	0.041*	0.050*
Race/ethnicity				
Chicano	1.295*	--	--	--
Black	1.405*	--	--	--
White**				
Sex				
Female	0.947	0.974	0.955	0.885
Male**				
Age				
Young (18-20)	1.190*	1.037	1.335	1.297
Old (41+)	0.823	0.780	0.906	0.825
Middle-aged**				
Offense type				
Homicide	0.348*	0.246*	0.657	0.288*
Assault	0.831	0.914	0.834	0.797
Burglary	0.823	0.873	0.900	0.762
Theft	1.094	1.363	1.117	0.860
Auto theft	2.556*	2.796*	2.485*	2.356*
Forgery	0.248*	0.307*	<.001	0.345*
Rape	1.101	1.167	0.893	1.249
Narcotics	0.363*	0.453	0.206*	0.363*
Other felony	0.363*	0.377*	0.247*	0.487*
Robbery**				
Evidence				
Firearm	0.694	0.955	0.348	0.552
No Firearm**				
Possession	1.460*	1.492	2.847*	1.033
No possession				
Offense severity				
(1 = high, 9 = low)	0.904*	0.878*	0.921	0.935
Duration***	−0.128*	−0.107*	−0.139*	−0.159*

TABLE 5.1   Continued

Variables	All Race/Ethnicities	Whites	Chicanos	Blacks
	B. Prosecution Denial of Complaint			
% of all events:	13.9%	11.5%	13.8%	18.1%
(Constant)	0.019*	0.020*	0.019*	0.029*
Race/ethnicity				
Chicano	1.251*	--	--	--
Black	1.638*	--	--	--
White**				
Sex				
Female	1.055	1.102	0.991	1.021
Male**				
Age				
Young (18–20)	0.951	0.995	1.102	0.761
Old (41+)	0.933	0.876	0.711	1.117
Middle-aged**				
Offense type				
Homicide	0.557*	0.360	0.659	0.720
Assault	1.109	1.145	1.154	1.035
Burglary	0.558*	0.507*	0.660	0.554*
Theft	1.072	0.961	1.291	1.054
Auto theft	1.742*	2.359*	1.735	1.180
Forgery	0.192*	0.238*	<.001	0.199*
Rape	0.708	0.741	0.209	0.979
Narcotics	0.717*	0.792	0.576	0.678
Other felony	0.728*	0.750	0.778	0.660
Robbery**				
Evidence				
Firearm	0.734	0.732	0.816	0.580
No firearm**				
Possession	2.312*	2.150*	3.190*	2.202*
No Possession**				
Offense severity				
(1 = high, 9 = low)	0.904*	0.921*	0.943	0.965
Duration***	−0.084	−0.083	−0.075	−0.089

(continued)

TABLE 5.1   Continued

Variables	All Race/Ethnicities	Whites	Chicanos	Blacks
	C. Lower or Superior Court			
% of all events:	75.6%	79.7%	74.2%	69.2%
(Constant)	0.007*	0.007*	0.007*	0.007*
Race/ethnicity				
Chicano	1.092*	--	--	--
Black	0.909*	--	--	--
White**				
Sex				
Female	1.041	1.056	0.994	1.036
Male**				
Age				
Young (18–20)	1.093*	1.147*	0.960	1.118
Old (41+)	0.989	0.885*	1.201*	1.140*
Middle–Aged**				
Offense type				
Homicide	0.698*	0.693*	0.798	0.634*
Assault	1.010	1.044	0.848	1.102
Burglary	1.069	1.115	0.970	1.043
Theft	1.059	1.031	0.975	1.197
Auto theft	1.117	1.289*	0.927	1.059
Forgery	0.919	0.944	0.930	0.920
Rape	0.968	0.964	0.996	0.887
Narcotics	0.607*	0.631*	0.489*	0.637*
Other felony	0.916	0.939	0.828	0.978
Robbery**				
Evidence				
Firearm	1.162	1.150	1.216	1.173
No firearm**				
Possession	1.187*	1.157*	1.156	1.265*
No possession**				
Offense severity				
(1 = high, 9 = low)	1.053*	1.045*	1.086*	1.033
Duration***	–0.0004*	–0.0003*	–0.0004	–0.0004*

*Significant at p = .05 without direction predicted.
**Reference category.
***Estimated parameter, not antilog. Time unit is days.

TABLE 5.2 Antilogs of Estimated Coefficients for Sixth or Later Shifts for Each Destination State.

Variables	All Race/Ethnicities	Whites	Chicanos	Blacks
Number of events:	1430	376	207	847
		A. Police Release		
% of all events:	9.8%	5.9%	7.2%	12.2%
(Constant)	0.013*	0.003*	0.085*	0.044*
Race/ethnicity				
Chicano	1.161	––	––	––
Black	2.221*	––	––	––
White**				
Sex				
Female	0.137*	0.886	<.001	0.001
Male**				
Age				
Young (18–20)	1.120	1.291	1.176	1.107
Old (41+)	0.364	0.971	1.621	0.155
Middle–aged**				
Offense type				
Homicide	7.606	0.031	****	****
Assault	1.897	1.385	****	2.020
Burglary	1.808	0.940	****	1.484
Theft	2.358	0.808	****	2.949
Auto theft	3.228*	0.271	****	4.425*
Forgery	0.796	0.002	<.001	1.364
Rape	2.780	0.001	<.001	2.609
Narcotics	2.279	1.245	0.336	2.303
Other felony	1.722	0.919	****	1.843
Robbery**				
Evidence				
Firearm	1.831	4.582	1.086	1.016
No firearm**				
Possession	0.675	0.296	****	0.815
No possession**				
Offense severity				
(1 = high, 9 = low)	0.955	1.275	0.857	0.887
Duration***	−0.257*	−0.206*	−0.314*	−0.262*

(continued)

TABLE 5.2   Continued

Variables	All Race/Ethnicities	Whites	Chicanos	Blacks
	B. Prosecution Denial of Complaint			
% of all events	15.9%	12.8%	17.9%	16.8%
(Constant)	0.019*	0.010*	0.129	0.026*
Race/ethnicity				
Chicano	1.368	--	--	--
Black	1.331	--	--	--
White**				
Sex				
Female	1.613	1.011	<.001	2.069*
Male**				
Age				
Young (18–20)	0.846	0.538	0.655	1.076
Old (41+)	1.094	1.597	<.001	1.058
Middle–aged**				
Offense type				
Homicide	1.950	1.796	0.616	****
Assault	2.147	4.907	0.671	4.219*
Burglary	0.678	2.132	1.041	0.632
Theft	1.894	8.473	2.080	1.865
Auto theft	2.951*	7.276	2.654	3.734*
Forgery	0.496	0.003	<.001	1.204
Rape	3.518*	32.670*	1.343	2.615
Narcotics	1.024	5.175	0.316	0.972
Other felony	1.547	1.652	0.577	1.932
Robbery**				
Evidence				
Firearm	1.106	5.577	2.355	0.663
No firearm**				
Possession	3.085*	2.893	6.869	3.130*
No possession**				
Offense severity				
(1 = high, 9 = low)	0.873*	0.852	0.678	0.853*
Duration***	–0.085*	–0.148*	–0.063*	–0.079*

TABLE 5.2 Continued

Variable	All Race/Ethnicities	White	Chicanos	Blacks
	C. Lower or Superior Court			
% of all events:	74.3%	81.4%	74.9%	71.1%
(Constant)	0.005*	0.006*	<.001*	0.005*
Race/ethnicity				
Chicano	0.972	——	——	——
Black	0.920	——	——	——
White**				
Sex				
Female	0.737*	0.566	8.797*	0.823
Male**				
Age				
Young (18–20)	0.860	0.938	0.594*	0.912
Old (41+)	1.337*	1.432	1.692	1.228
Middle–aged**				
Offense type				
Homicide	0.240	0.315	<.001	****
Assault	1.839*	1.770	2.699*	1.627
Burglary	0.904	0.728	1.344	0.769
Theft	0.910	0.836	0.643	0.834
Auto theft	0.980	0.778	1.592	0.831
Forgery	1.210	0.870	3.513	1.177
Rape	1.577	0.801	2.679	1.689
Narcotics	1.092	0.773	1.587	1.209
Other felony	1.372	1.134	4.147*	1.262
Robbery**				
Evidence				
Firearm	1.133	0.964	0.839	1.171
No firearm**				
Possession	0.791	0.907	0.487	0.744
No possession**				
Offense severity				
(1 = high, 9 = low)	1.124*	1.147*	1.405*	1.121*
Duration***	−0.0005	−0.0004	+0.0011	−0.0006

*Significant at p = .05 without direction predicted.
**Reference category.
***Estimated parameter, not antilog. Time unit is days.
****Removed from vector because of lack of variance.

parameters. This assumption has received a good deal of attention (e.g., Blumen et al., 1955; Coleman, 1964, 1973; and Tuma, 1976). Following Tuma (1976) and Tuma et al. (1979), the population homogeneity assumption is relaxed here to assume only that, in a manner analogous to the interpretation of parameter estimates in OLS regression analysis, the same rates of change apply to every individual with the same values on variables (e.g., female, Black, homicide arrest, etc.)

The time-stationarity assumption means that the parameters are constant over time. Nevertheless, it might be that rates of moving from one state to another *are* some specific function of time (Mayer, 1972; Tuma, 1976; Sørensen and Tuma, 1978; Felmlee, 1980). That is, causal relationships could change over time, resulting in rates which vary over the duration in a state (e.g., arrest). For example, transition rates will be different for cases which move quickly from arrest to disposition as compared with cases which take a long time to move from arrest to disposition. The duration in the state of arrest, then, can impact rates of changing to the disposition states.

Such duration dependence can be due to a variety of factors. The two most generally applicable factors suggest, first, that the effect of duration in a state (e.g., time spent in the criminal justice system between arrest and case disposition) could simply be a function of uncontrolled heterogeneity (Ginsberg, 1971). That is, variation in the individual rates not controlled for by other exogenous variables in the model could be visible as a duration effect. Accordingly, some degree of duration dependence is expected.

A second source of duration dependence, if it is negative in direction, is what McGinnis (1968) has called "cumulative inertia." This means that the rate of transition to a new state (analogous to the probability of moving in discrete time) declines monotonically as time spent in a state increases. Thus, for example, persons committed to prison for increasingly long periods might see less and less to gain in following the prison rules and much to gain in violating such rules (thereby making their prison stay more comfortable) and, as a consequence, be denied "good time" toward release, thereby increasing their length of time in incarceration. Similarly, a person who has been waiting a long time for case disposition could be less likely to have his or her case disposed of in the next instant of time than someone who was more recently arrested. Causes of such inertia include problems in building a strong case against the defendant, a decrease over time in public concern with a particular offense, and other factors which make the rate of leaving a state decline with increased time spent in it.

Inclusion of both the population heterogeneity and time-dependence modifications into the Markov model (Tuma et al., 1979), as well as the assumption of a log-linear functional form, results in a continuous-time, finite-state, multivariate, stochastic model of the form:

$$r_{jk}(t) = e^{(\underline{\alpha}_{jk}\underline{X}) + (\underline{\beta}_{jk}\underline{Y})t} \tag{2}$$

where $\underline{\alpha}_{jk}$ and $\underline{\beta}_{jk}$ are vectors of parameters to be estimated. The rate of change from state j to state k is both multivariate and time-dependent, with the vector Y accounting for the time-dependence.

The parameters of RATE models are estimated through use of maximum-likelihood estimation (Tuma et al., 1979). Thus, those parameter values that make the observations in the sample most likely are chosen. Among other advantages, this estimation technique permits a satisfactory solution to the problem of data collection ceasing before all cases have moved into their destination states (the exclusion of such observations, which are said to be "censored," has been shown to result in errors of inference), and has good properties for large samples under fairly general conditions and for small samples with moderate degrees of censoring. Furthermore, these good properties are retained under any monotonic transformations, so estimators of rates can be used to form estimators for expected durations in a variety of outcome states (Tuma and Hannan, 1978; Tuma et al., 1979). In addition, maximum-likelihood estimators can be obtained for most stochastic processes.

ANALYSES AND DISCUSSION

For this illustrative example, instantaneous rates of transition from the state of arrest to the states which comprise the points of case dispositions are modeled. These transitions were chosen because they represent the first stage in the processing of criminal defendants, following entrance into the criminal justice system. The rates to each disposition point (police release, prosecution denial of complaint, and lower or superior court) are modeled separately for each processing of the defendant, or what is called each "shift." That is, in a manner appropriate for the reconceptualization of recidivism suggested here, the first through fifth processings of an individual are analyzed separately, with the sixth through fifteenth shifts combined[11] (reflecting the lesser frequency with which such processings occur). In addition, both the direct effects of race/ethnicity on these rates (through inclusion of racial/ethnic memberships as exogenous variables) and the interaction effects of race/ethnicity with other legal and extralegal factors (through separate analyses for each race/ethnicity) are assessed. In the interests of parsimony, full results are reported here only for the first shift and the sixth and later shifts (with the latter combined into one

TABLE 5.3   Antilogs of Estimated Coefficients for Blacks and Chicanos*
Controlling for Offense Variables, Age, and Sex, (First
through sixth or later shifts)

Variable	Shift1	Shift2	Shift3	Shift4	Shift5	Shift6+
			Police Release			
Black	1.405**	1.862**	1.757**	1.769**	1.948**	2.221**
Chicano	1.295**	1.459**	1.580**	1.268	0.919	1.161
Estimated						
rate***	0.00119	0.00108	0.00106	0.00125	0.00142	0.00139
			Prosecution Denial of Complaint			
Black	1.638**	1.614**	1.652**	1.602**	1.683**	1.331
Chicano	1.251**	1.495**	1.365**	1.454**	1.483**	1.368
Estimated						
rate***	0.00159	0.00153	0.00154	0.00166	0.00174	0.00226
			Lower or Superior Court			
Black	0.909**	0.865**	0.940	0.947	0.931	0.920
Chicano	1.092**	0.997	0.991	0.940	0.950	0.972
Estimated						
rate***	0.00864	0.00870	0.00924	0.00952	0.00934	0.01057
N of events	10,892	5,552	4,805	4,171	2,167	1,430

*Whites are reference category.
**Significant at p = .05 without direction predicted.
***Time unit is days.

analysis). Direct effects of race/ethnicity on all shifts are also presented
(see Table 5.3) enabling comparisons of these effects across shifts, although the effects of control variables included in the models are not
reported.

Table 5.1 presents the antilogs of the estimated effects for the first
shifts to each destination state, and Table 5.2 presents the same information for sixth or later shifts. Antilogs of the estimated parameters are
reported rather than the parameters themselves because they are more
easily interpretable. Both the overall model (including the main effects of
race/ethnicity) and separate analyses for each race/ethnicity are presented
in both tables. All of the variables, with the exception of offense severity
and duration, are dummy variables. The antilogs of dummy variables are
interpreted as percentage increases (if greater than 1.0) or decreases (if less
than 1.0) in the rate of transition due to the effect of that variable, relative
to the reference category. Values for the offense severity variable range

from one through nine. The antilog for this variable reflects the increase or decrease in the rate of moving attributable to a one-unit change in the value of this variable. The estimated parameter itself, rather than the antilog of the parameter, is reported for the duration variable. As was discussed earlier, this effect has several sources, the most commonly applicable of which are cumulative inertia (i.e., rates of moving from one state to another decrease the longer one stays in the origin state) and uncontrolled heterogeneity (i.e., variation not controlled for by the set of exogenous variables in the model). The duration effects are consistently negative, meaning that the rate of transition from arrest to disposition decreases as the length of time in the state of arrest increases.

Table 5.1 demonstrates that Chicanos have significantly higher rates of transition from arrest to disposition than do Whites in their first shifts, regardless of the point of disposition. Similarly, Blacks move from arrest to release by both the police and the prosecutor more swiftly than do Whites in their first shift. Interpretation of these findings without knowledge of the type of defense attorney and of the defendant's pretrial detention status is difficult. One plausible explanation, though, is that Whites are better able than are Blacks and Chicanos to reward nonenforcement of the law (Chambliss and Seidman, 1971), while Blacks and Chicanos can be processed without creating any undue strains on the organizations which comprise the criminal justice system (and, thus, more quickly) if, for example, they are less likely than are Whites to retain private attorneys.

Of the other defendant characteristics, sex has no effect on transition rates, but age does have some effect. Being young, relative to being middle-aged, increases the rate of transition from arrest to both police release and court disposition for the model combining all race/ethnicities, as well as for Whites whose cases are disposed of by the court. Interestingly, for those persons disposed of by the court, the effect of being over 40 (relative to being middle-aged) varies depending on one's racial/ethnic membership. That is, older Whites have their cases disposed of more slowly than do middle-aged Whites, while older Blacks and Chicanos are processed more quickly than are middle-aged Blacks and Chicanos. Again, it is difficult to speculate on reasons for this finding without knowledge of the type of defense counsel; but if older Whites are most likely to retain private counsel, then this could slow the rate at which their cases are disposed of by the court.

For the model including the main effects of race/ethnicity, an arrest for auto theft results in speedier transitions to police and prosecution dispositions (relative to robbery), while arrests for homicide, forgery, and narcotics result in slower releases by the police and, along with burglary arrests, to slower disposition by the prosecutor. Once the case proceeds to the court, however, the only arrest offenses which significantly affect the rate are homicide and narcotics, both of which make the case take longer to reach disposition.

Interestingly, separate analyses for each race/ethnicity demonstrate that Chicanos arrested for narcotics offenses (relative to the reference category, robbery) are released by the police more quickly than are Whites or Blacks, although persons arrested for narcotics are released more slowly in general than are persons arrested for robbery. This finding that Chicanos are arrested and quickly processed and released for narcotics offenses suggests, however, the possibility that they are especially likely to be picked up for questioning concerning the distribution and sale of narcotics or for suspicion of engaging in such activities, with little grounds for the arrest and, as a consequence, released before the case reaches the prosecutor. Questions concerning differential processing, however, require examination of criminal processing histories.

Since this discussion is intended simply to illustrate the uses and interpretations of RATE models, a detailed discussion of the results of analyses of the second through fifth shifts is omitted. An examination of analyses for sixth and later shifts (combined) demonstrates the effects of exogenous variables on rates of transition from arrest to case disposition for persons who have been processed by the criminal justice system six or more times within a three-year period. Such persons are, then, fast shifters. Table 5.2 reports these results for both the overall model (including main effects of race/ethnicity) and separate analyses for each racial/ethnic group. Interestingly, the only significant main effect of race/ethnicity is the faster release of Blacks by the police. Thus, controlling for other relevant factors, most main effects of race/ethnicity are insignificant by the time a person has undergone processing by the criminal justice system six or more times. While this is explained in part by the reduced number of cases in these analyses as compared with those for first shifters (making statistical significance more difficult to attain), it may also reflect the loss of any leniency accorded Whites during earlier processings.

The effects of sex do, however, become significant, with females released by the police and disposed of by the court more slowly than males. Controlling for offense type, offense severity, evidence, and the defendant's age and race/ethnicity, then, women who quickly reappear in the criminal justice process are treated differently than are women who take a longer time to reappear in the criminal justice system. In addition, sex interacts with race/ethnicity such that Chicanas (female Chicanos) have their cases disposed of by the court more quickly than do their male counterparts, and cases are denied by the prosecutor faster when they involve Black women rather than Black men. That this finding exists for sixth or later shifts and not for first shifts strongly suggests the need for further research on differential processing by both race/ethnicity and sex across court processings, using techniques which allow for the dynamic nature of such processings.

Generally, the effect of duration, while consistently negative and significant, is largest for movement to the police destination, smaller for prosecution, and smallest for court destination. This trend holds for each race/ethnicity as well as for the combined model for the first shift and for sixth or later shifts. "Cumulative inertia" (McGinnis, 1968) can explain these negative duration effects, as cases which are not quickly disposed of by the police or prosecutor take increasingly longer to reach disposition. Uncertainty concerning the ability of the prosecutor to win the case, a decrease in interest in the case as newer and potentially more important cases enter the criminal justice process, and other causes of delay thus result in cases which are not immediately disposed of taking increasingly longer to reach disposition. In addition to cumulative inertia, unexplained heterogeneity (Ginsberg, 1971) could be a source of duration dependence. That is, variables which are important predictors of police release and, to a lesser extent, of prosecution release through denial of complaint may be missing from these models. Thus, for example, the context in which the arrest occurred could impact case dispositions, particularly by the police and prosecutor.

The finding noted above, that most of the effects of race/ethnicity in the analyses for the first shift become insignificant by the sixth or later shifts, is deserving of some attention. Accordingly, Table 5.3 reports the effects of being Black and Chicano, relative to being White, on rates of transition to the three destination states, for all shifts. All of the exogenous variables reported in the first two tables were controlled for in these analyses, although only the effects of the race/ethnicity variables are shown.

As is clear from Table 5.3, race/ethnicity significantly affects transition rates to police release and prosecution for most shifts. The antilogs of the effects for these two destination states are generally greater than 1.0, meaning that Blacks and Chicanos are processed more swiftly by the police and prosecutor than are Whites. This finding holds consistently for the first through fifth shifts to the prosecutor for both Blacks and Chicanos, and Blacks are released by the police much more quickly than are Whites for *all* shifts. Furthermore, the difference between Chicanos and Whites remains significant until the fourth shift. Interestingly, this pattern is reversed when the destination state is the court. At this point, both first- and second-shift Whites are processed more speedily than are Blacks. Aside from these latter two situations and the slower processing of first-shift

Whites than Chicanos, no significant main effects of race/ethnicity are visible when the destination state is court disposition.

Such findings suggest that Chicanos—and especially Blacks—are particularly likely to be arrested by the police with little grounds for the arrest and, as a result, are quickly released. Blacks and Chicanos might also be more likely to be arrested in an effort by police to garner information concerning criminal activities they are suspected to be knowledgeable of and then promptly released. When defendants are not released by the police but, instead, their cases continue on to the prosecutor, both Blacks' and Chicanos' cases are disposed of by the prosecutor for reason of "denial of complaint" more speedily than are Whites'. Again, this is controlling for offense type, offense severity, evidence, sex, and age.

Furthermore, the effects of being Black or Chicano on these rates are larger for later, as compared with earlier, shifts. That is, the speed with which Blacks and Chicanos (as compared to Whites) are processed increases with each reappearance of the same person in the criminal justice system. This implies that Blacks and Chicanos who are known to the police and prosecutor may be particularly vulnerable to arrest. It does not, however, necessarily indicate any greater criminality on their parts, particularly since Blacks and Chicanos are quickly released by the police or have their cases denied by the prosecutor. Rather, it suggests vulnerability to possible police bias. Accordingly, Blacks and Chicanos who are known to the police might be more likely to be arrested for suspicious activities (which would not be noticed were they not already known to the police), or for questioning in an attempt by police to garner information. Although the actual situations in which the arrests occurred are unknown, rendering any explanations speculative, these findings could reflect greater vulnerability of Blacks and Chicanos to the biases of social control agents (Burke and Turk, 1975) and greater power of Whites than of Blacks and Chicanos to reward nonenforcement of the law (Chambliss and Seidman, 1971).

CONCLUSIONS

That the criminal justice system is processual is not new. Nevertheless, processing models are rare in criminological research, largely as a result of the lack of data constituting processing histories of criminal defendants and of methodological techniques for analyzing such data. This chapter describes one such modeling technique appropriate for the study of the criminal processing of individual defendants in continuous-time and provides an illustrative application through analysis of the processing of defendants from arrest to point of disposition. The model chosen is one of a class of multivariate, finite-state, continuous-time, stochastic models. Use of such a model allows us to trace the actual transitions of individuals from one stage of the criminal justice process to the next, with explicit consideration of the interrelatedness of potential outcomes in processing decisions, over a period of time.

It is argued here that dynamic modeling of longitudinal data both enables us to answer existing questions concerning criminal justice processing (e.g., the existence and manifestations of differential treatment by race/ethnicity) and suggests new questions and novel approaches to old questions. For example, analysis of longitudinal criminal justice processing data foists a reconceptualization of recidivism on the researcher. This reconceptualization involves treating recidivism as an *aspect* of criminal justice processing, rather than as a defendant status. Accordingly, attention is focused on whether or not rates of transitions for initial and later processings of the *same* individuals differ. Using data which form criminal processing histories of individuals, separate analyses are performed on each shift, or processing of the same individual. Within each of these shifts, main and interaction effects of race/ethnicity and other exogenous variables on rates of moving from arrest to case disposition are examined. Differences are found among racial/ethnic groups across shifts to each of the three outcome states (police release, prosecution denial of complaint, and court disposition).

The call for further research, which typifies research conclusions, is particularly strong here. Criminal processing histories are available (although the need for more complete histories certainly exists) and can be fruitfully utilized in dynamic analyses of criminal justice processing. With such data sets and with methodological techniques such as the RATE model explicated here, formal models of criminal justice processing can be developed and tested, and the effects of factors such as race/ethnicity on processing decisions can be readily assessed.

NOTES

1. See also Tuma (1976), Hannan et al. (1977), Tuma and Hannan (1978), Sorensen and Tuma (1978), and Hannan and Tuma (1979).

2. Even studies which attempt to model recidivism through use of failure rates (e.g., Bloom, 1979; Gaines, 1981; Harris and Moitra, 1978) treat recidivists and nonrecidivists as different groups. Greenberg (1978) further subdivides the population of released prisoners into three groups (permanently law-abiding, nonviolators lacking commitment to abstention from crime, and violators who may be officially classified as recidivists).

3. A potential problem here is the determination of whether the first processing of an individual in a data set reflects the first time the person has actually entered the

criminal justice system. This becomes problematic only if censored observations are not randomly distributed across racial/ethnic groups. Knowledge of the individual's prior criminal record provides useful information, but in the data base used here, such information is not recorded for cases which do not reach court disposition. Thus, information on observations prior to the start of data collection is not available. Such observations are said to be left-censored. Generally, left-censoring should reduce differences between first and later processings, resulting in more conservative tests of significance (i.e., statistically significant effects will be more difficult to attain).

4. Ideally, sampling should be based solely on the origin state (arrest) with no consideration of disposition. Since there is no reason to suspect that slow cases (i.e., cases taking a long time to move from arrest to disposition) are not distributed randomly in time, however, the assumption can be made that the system is in a state of relative equilibrium. Consequently, left-censoring is not expected to bias parameter estimates.

5. Age is categorized as 18-20 years of age (approximately 20 percent of the sample), 21-40 (approximately 70 percent of the sample), and 41 or older (approximately 10 percent of the sample).

6. The offense categorizations used here roughly follow those used by the State of California Departments of Justice and of Corrections, with some adjustments made for the relative frequencies of these offenses in the sample analyzed. The "rape" category includes only felonious rapes; other sex offenses are subsumed under the category "other felonies."

7. The severity scale used here ranges in value from one through nine, where one is the most severe. It is a collapsed version of the severity scale used by the State of California, Department of Justice.

8. The two indicators of evidence are possession (of a controlled substance, burglary tools, etc.) and use of a firearm in committing the offense.

9. In a related study currently in progress, these data are merged with cohort data for the *same* criminal cases obtained from the State of California, Department of Corrections. Incorporation of this second data set, which includes information on the dates of commitment to and release from incarceration, enlarges the scope of the criminal justice processing examined, extending it from arrest through release from incarceration.

10. Related to this, the need arises to state the explicit dependence of these rates on the observable, exogenous variables. A log-linear relation between each transition rate and the exogenous variables is assumed here. This relationship was chosen because it has the advantage of constraining each rate to be positive for each individual, and by definition rates of change must be positive.

11. Ideally, each shift should be examined separately. Of the 450,000 criminal cases in the data base employed here, however, only 80 represent Chicanos in seventh or later shifts, and only about 20 percent of these represent shifts to police and prosecution dispositions, resulting in unstable parameter estimates. As a result, sixth or later processings have been collapsed. While this could result in slightly biased coefficients since, at least conceptually, these shifts should not be combined, such a procedure reflects some improvement on traditional categorizations of recidivists.

REFERENCES

BLOOM, H. S. (1979) "Evaluating human services and correctional programs by modeling the timing of recidivism." Soc. Methods and Research 8: 179-208.

BLUMEN, I., M. KOGAN, and P. J. McCARTHY (1955) The Industrial Mobility of Labor as a Probability Process. Ithaca, NY: Cornell Univ. Press.

BREWER, D. (1979) Race and Prison Terms. Southern California Research Group State of California Department of Corrections.

BURKE, P. J. and A. T. TURK (1975) "Factors affecting post-arrest dispositions: a model for analysis." Social Problems 22: 313-332.

CARRO, J. (1980) "Hispanics underrepresented as criminal justice professionals." U.S. Department of Justice: Justice Assistance News 1: 2, 7.

CHAMBLISS, W. J. and R. B. SEIDMAN (1971) Law, Order, and Power. Reading, MA: Addison-Wesley.

COLEMAN, J. S. (1973) The Mathematics of Collective Action. Chicago: Aldine.

––– (1964) Introduction to Mathematical Sociology. New York: Free Press.

FELMLEE, D. H. (1980) "The dynamics of women's job mobility." Presented at the American Sociological Association annual meetings, New York, August 27-31.

GAINES, J. A. (1981) "Modeling recidivism times: comment on Bloom." Soc. Methods and Research 10: 112-118.

GINSBERG, R. B. (1971) "Semi-Markov processes and mobility." J. of Mathematical Sociology 1: 233-262.

GREENBERG, D. F. (1978) "Recidivism as radioactive decay." J. of Research in Crime and Delinquency 15: 124-125.

HAGAN, J. (1974) "Extra-legal attributes and criminal sentencing: an assessment of a sociological viewpoint." Law and Society 8: 357-383.

HANNAN, M. T. and N. B. TUMA (1979) "Methods for temporal analysis." Annual Rev. of Sociology 5: 303-328.

––– and T. GROENEVELD (1977) "Income and marital events: evidence from an income-maintenance experiment." Amer. J. of Sociology 82: 1186-1211.

HARRIS, C. M. and S. D. MOITRA (1978) "Improved statistical techniques for the measurement of recidivism." J. of Research in Crime and Delinquency 15: 194-213.

LaFREE, G. D. (1980) "The effect of sexual stratification by race on official reactions to rape." Amer. Soc. Rev. 45: 842-854.

MAYER, T. F. (1972) "Models of intragenerational mobility," in J. Berger, M. Zelditch, Jr., and B. Anderson (eds.) Sociological Theories in Progress, Vol. II. Boston: Houghton Mifflin.

McGINNIS, R. (1968) "A stochastic model of social mobility." Amer. Soc. Rev. 33: 712-722.

MOORE, J. W., R. GARCIA, C. GARCIA, L. CERDA, and F. VALENCIA (1978) Homeboys: Gangs, Drugs, and Prison in the Barrios of Los Angeles. Philadelphia: Temple Univ. Press.

SISSONS, P. L. (1979) The Hispanic Experience of Criminal Justice. New York: Hispanic Research Center, Fordham University.

SØRENSEN, A. B. and N. B. TUMA (1978) Labor Market Structures and Job Mobility. Institute for Research on Poverty Discussion Paper.

TUMA, N. B. (1976) "Rewards, resources, and rate of mobility: a nonstationary, multivariate, stochastic model." Amer. Soc. Rev. 41: 338-360.

――― and D. CROCKFORD (1976) Invoking RATE. Stanford: Department of Sociology, Stanford University. (unpublished)

TUMA, N. B. and M. T. HANNAN (1978) "Approaches to the censoring problem in analysis of event histories," in K. Schuessler (ed.) Sociological Methodology, 1979. San Francisco: Jossey-Bass.

――― and L. T. GROENEVELD (1979) "Dynamic analysis of event histories." Amer. J. of Sociology 84: 820-854.

WOLFGANG, M. E., R. M. FIGLIO, and T. SELLIN (1972) Delinquency in a Birth Cohort. Chicago: Univ. of Chicago Press.

Michael Hout
University of Arizona

6

USING UNIFORM ASSOCIATION MODELS
An Example from Delinquency Research

The general log-linear model for the analysis of cross-classified data (Goodman, 1970, 1972; Fienberg, 1980) makes no assumptions about the level of measurement of the variables in the cross-classification. In many instances this feature of the general log-linear model is an advantage because it provides a rigorous method for analyzing data that are not scalable or are of unknown scalability. In other instances, substantial a priori evidence of order (if not scale) is available to the researcher. Suppression of such information is an inefficient use of the data.

The uniform association model and its generalizations provide an efficient method of incorporating information about order into the analysis of cross-classified data (see Goodman, 1979a, 1979b; Haberman, 1974; Duncan, 1979; Clogg, forthcoming for rigorous development of this and other models for ordered data). The model captures each two-way association with a single parameter that shifts the distribution of one variable upward or downward as the other variable is moved up or down. The model can be generalized to estimate partial uniform association and other forms of higher-order interaction (Clogg, forthcoming), but these developments are beyond the scope of this chapter.

The uniform association model derives its name from a condition it places on the odds ratios for 2x2 subtables of a two-way table formed from pairs of adjacent rows and columns:

$$\theta_{ij} = F_{ij}F_{i+1,j+1}/F_{i+1,j}F_{i,j+1} = \theta$$

for $i = 1$ to $I-1$ and $j = 1$ to $J-1$. In other words, the model implies that differences among the elements of "the basic set of interactions" (Goodman, 1969, 1979a) are not statistically significant—that is, that the elements are "uniform."

This chapter gives examples of uniform association in a two-way and three-way table. My approach to the data is more exploratory than usual. I begin with the results of an analysis that assumes no order among categories and proceed inductively. Normally the order among the categories is an important part of a study's design. If order is known, the analysis can begin with uniform association, bypassing other models. I use the inductive approach here to link uniform association to more familiar models and to show how uniform association can be recognized in the results of other kinds of analysis.

DATA

The data for this example are from Jensen (1972: Table 2), who reported a 3x3x3 cross-classification of self-reported delinquent acts by number of delinquent friends by attitude toward breaking the law. The data are from the Richmond (California) Youth Study. Only nonblack males are included. First, I shall analyze the two-way association of friends and acts. The frequencies for this two-way association as reconstituted from Jensen's percentages are in Table 6.1. After the two-way analysis, I shall turn to the three-way table.

ANALYSIS OF FRIENDS BY ACTS

Results from the General Log-Linear Model

The first model fit to Table 6.1 is the model of independence that fits just the marginals for friends ($u_{F(i)}$) and acts ($u_{A(j)}$):

$$LN(F_{ij}) = u + u_{F(i)} + u_{A(j)} \qquad [1]$$

where $\Sigma\, u_{F(i)} = \Sigma\, u_{A(j)} = 0$.

The expected frequencies under the model of independence are shown in the second column of numbers in Table 6.1. The association between friends and acts is significant, as indicted by the poor fit of the model of independence ($L^2 = 184.00$; df = 4; $p < .001$) where L^2 is the likelihood ratio statistic:

$$L^2 = 2 \sum_{i}^{I} \sum_{j}^{J} f_{ij} LN(f_{ij}/F_{ij})$$

TABLE 6.1   Self-Reported Delinquent Acts by Number of Delinquent Friends

Number of Delinquent:			Expected	
Friends	*Acts*	*Observed*	*Indep.*	*LL/UA*
0	0	391	300.6	388.1
	1	106	135.2	112.6
	2+	47	108.2	43.3
1 – 2	0	135	150.3	137.6
	1	84	67.6	77.1
	2+	53	54.1	57.3
3+	0	74	149.2	74.2
	1	80	67.1	80.4
	2+	116	53.7	115.4

SOURCE: Jensen (1972).

which is distributed approximately as chi-square with $(I-1)(J-1)$ degrees of freedom.

Comparing the observed frequencies with those expected under independence shows that the largest departures from independence are at the corners of the table. Among youths with no delinquent friends there are more who report no delinquent acts and fewer who report two or more delinquent acts than expected under independence. Conversely, among youths with three or more delinquent friends, there are fewer than expected reporting no delinquent acts and more than expected reporting two or more delinquent acts.

This pattern of large departures from independence concentrated at the corners of the two-way table can be seen clearly in the parameters of the saturated model which adds a parameter of association for each cell $(u_{FA(ij)})$ to the model of independence:

$$LN(F_{ij}) = u + u_{F(i)} + u_{A(j)} + u_{FA(ij)} \qquad [2]$$

$$\text{where } \sum_i u_{FA(ij)} = \sum_j u_{FA(ij)} = 0$$

The parameter estimates for this model are in Table 6.2. The saturated model uses all nine degrees of freedom in the 3x3 table, so it reporduces the observed frequencies exactly. Equations 1 and 2 are the only two models offered by the usual hierarchical modeling method for the analysis of two-way tables. However, other models are possible once constraints on the $u_{FA(ij)}$ are considered.

TABLE 6.2   Parameter Estimates for Saturated Log-Linear Model for
Delinquent Acts (A) by Delinquent Friends (F)

Effect		Level		
		1	*2*	*3*
Grand Mean		4.58		
Marginals:	A	.48	-.09	-.39
	F	.25	-.15	-.20
Two-Way: AF	1j	.66	-.07	-.59
	2j	⁻.01	.08	⁻.07
	3j	⁻.65	⁻.01	.66

Linear-by-Linear and Uniform Association Models

Notice that the four $u_{12(ij)}$ for the corners of the table are very close in absolute value (.66, -.59, -.65, .66) and that the other five are close to zero. Consider a model that constrains the corner parameters to take exactly the same absolute value and the other five to be exactly zero:

$$LN(F_{ij}) = u + u_{F(i)} + u_{A(j)} + a(i-2)(j-2)$$ [3]

Haberman (1979: 385-387) calls this the "linear-by-linear interaction" (LL) model. This model fits the friends-by-acts data very well ($L^2 = 1.71$; df = 3; p > .50). The LL parameter is $a = .66$. The association between friends and acts is captured by this single parameter. No additional parameters are needed because to pass a chi-square test for significant improvement over the LL model (at the .05 level), a two parameter model would have to reduce L^2 by 3.84 or more, and L^2 for the LL model is only 1.71.

The LL model can be interpreted by taking the middle category on friends (one or two delinquent friends) as a reference point. The $u_{A(j)}$ column marginal parameters reflect the expected distribution of acts within this reference row. The LL parameter shifts the expected distribution of delinquent acts for youths with no delinquent friends in the direction of no delinquent acts by adding a to the log of the frequency that would otherwise be expected in the first column of that row and subtracting a from the log of the frequency that would otherwise be expected in the third column of that row (i.e., by adding a to cell [1,1] and subtracting a from cell [1,3]). Similarly, the LL parameter shifts the expected distribution of delinquent acts in the direction of two or more

TABLE 6.3   Parameterization of the LL and UA Models

Friends	Acts			Acts		
	0	*1*	*2+*	*0*	*1*	*2+*
	Linear-by-Linear			Uniform Association		
0	a	0	−a	0	0	0
1 − 2	0	0	0	0	b	2b
3+	−a	0	a	0	2b	4b

acts for youths with three or more delinquent friends by subtracting *a* from cell [3,1] and adding *a* to cell [3,3].

The LL model can be transformed by taking a different row as reference. In particular, if the first row is taken as referent, the following model is obtained:

$$LN(F_{ij}) = u + u_{1(i)} + u_{2(j)} + b(i-1)(j-1). \qquad [4]$$

This is the uniform association (UA) model (Goodman, 1979a, 1979b; Duncan, 1979). It is equivalent to the LL model (Goodman, 1979a); therefore the fit is the same ($L^2 = 1.71$; df = 3; p > .50). Expected frequencies for this model are shown in the last column of Table 6.1. Table 6.3 compares the parameterization of the association in the 3x3 table under the two models. Estimates of the parameters in equation 4 are in Table 6.4. Note that *b* = .66. This is the same value as was obtained for *a* in the LL model. This is not a coincidence. These parameters will always have the same value because the distances between adjacent categories in the two models are the same. The models differ solely in the specification of the reference category. This difference is reflected in the different values of the marginal effects terms ($u_{F(i)}$ and $u_{A(j)}$).

The interpretation of the UA parameter is similar to that of the LL parameter. The UA parameter regulates how much the distribution of delinquent acts is shifted upward or downward as the number of delinquent friends increases or decreases. The analogy to the regression coefficient is compelling (Duncan, 1979), but there is an important difference between the UA model and the regression model. The regression model predicts a unique value of the dependent variable for each value of the independent variable. In contrast, the UA model predicts the distribution of the dependent variable across its designated categories at each level of the independent variable.

TABLE 6.4   Parameter Estimates for Uniform Association Model for Delinquent Acts (A) by Delinquent Friends (F)

		Level		
Effect		*1*	*2*	*3*
Grand Mean		4.58		
Marginals:	A	1.14	-.09	-1.05
	F	.90	-.14	.76
Uniform Association (b)		.66		

To elaborate on the mechanics of the UA model, look to the reference category (zero delinquent friends). The column marginal effects reflect the distribution of expected log-frequencies for each column of the first row. This distribution is shifted toward more delinquent acts in the second and third rows by the UA parameter (b). The quantity b is added to the grand mean (u) and the row $2(u_{F(2)})$ and column 2 ($u_{A(2)}$) marginal effects to obtain $LN(F_{22})$, and $2b$ is added to the grand mean and marginal effects to obtain $LN(F_{23})$. The distribution of the third row is obtained in the same way. The quantity $2b$ is added to the second cell in the third row to obtain $LN(F_{32})$, and $4b$ is added to the third cell in the row to obtain $LN(F_{33})$. In this way the UA parameter shifts the distribution of delinquent acts in the direction of more acts with each increase in the number of delinquent friends.

The implications of the UA model for the odds on delinquent behavior is shown in Figure 6.1. The lines in the figure connect the expected odds; the squares locate the observed odds. The odds on one delinquent act (relative to none) increases linearly with the number of delinquent friends when plotted on log-log coordinates. The slope of the line is b = .66. Likewise, the effect of friends on the odds on repeat offenses (two or more delinquent acts relative to one) is parallel to the effect on one act—that is, the expected log-odd increase with a slope of b = .66.

As mentioned above, UA is so called because it constrains the odds ratios for 2x2 subtables formed from adjacent categories to all take the same value. This value is the antilog of b (i.e., b is the value of all four log-odds ratios). This characteristic of the model is shown clearly in Table 6.5, which presents both observed and expected log-odds ratios. A substantial range of observed values is covered by the single value b without significant deterioration of fit of model to data. The observed log-odds ratios vary from .35 to .83, while b = .66 is the expected value for all four

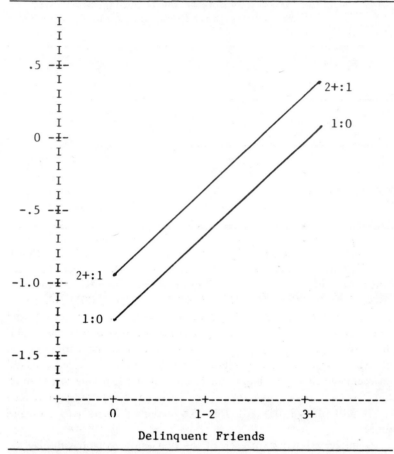

Figure 6.1 Log-Odds on Delinquent Acts Expected Under Uniform Association by Number of Delinquent Friends

log-odds ratios. This result suggests that unless the sample is very large, examining the observed odds ratios may not give much information about whether the UA model will or will not fit.

ANALYSIS OF THE THREE-WAY TABLE

The first column of numbers in Table 6.6 is the three-way cross-classification of delinquent acts (A) by delinquent friends (F) by definitions favorable to breaking the law (L) as reconstituted from Jensen's (1972: Table 2) percentages. The categories of L are (U) unfavorable, (N) neutral,

TABLE 6.5   Observed Log-Odds Ratios and Those Expected Under
             Uniform Association for Delinquent Acts by Delinquent
             Friends

		ij		
	11	12	21	22
Observed	.83	.35	.55	.83
Expected	.66	.66	.66	.66

and (F) favorable toward breaking the law. The other columns of Table
6.6 are frequencies expected under four models. The fit of these and other
models is shown in Table 6.7.

The first five models are those that would normally be fit when
following the procedures outlined by Goodman (1972), Fienberg (1980),
and others for the analysis of hierarchical models. The model of independence (M1) fits the three sets of univariate marginals but no two-way
associations. M1 does not fit ($L^2 = 370.37$; df = 20; p < .001). Adding the
association between the two independent variables in the analysis (F and
L) improves over M1 but does not produce an acceptable fit ($L_2 = 228.45$;
df = 16; p < .001). Adding the effects of friends and definitions on
behavior one at a time produces a similar result: improved but still
unacceptable fit ($L_2 = 44.45$ and 124.51; df = 12; p < .001). When all
three two-way associations are included (M5), an acceptable fit is obtained
($L^2 = 6.01$; df = 8; p > .50). Table 6.8 presents the parameter estimates
for M5.

Parameter estimates for each of the two-way associations display the
patterns found in Table 6.2—that is, large positive coefficients at the
extremes of the main diagonal, large negative coefficients at the extremes
of the reverse diagonal, and near-zero coefficients elsewhere. Substantively, these patterns mean that there are strong positive associations
among the youths' behavior, their friends' behavior, and their definitions
conducive to breaking the law. Jensen (1972) arrived at the same conclusion.

The similarity between the pattern of two-way association parameters
and the linear-by-linear interaction (LL) pattern discussed above suggests
that the data might be well described by a model that included a UA
parameter for each two-way association. Such a model takes the form:

$$LN(F_{ijk}) = u + u_{F(i)} + u_{A(j)} + u_{L(k)} + b_{FA}(i-1)(j-1)$$

$$+ b_2(i-1)(k-1) + b_3(j-1)(k-1) \qquad [5]$$

TABLE 6.6 Delinquent Acts by Delinquent Friends by Attitude Toward
Breaking the Law: Observed and Expected Frequencies

L	F	A	Observed	Expected Under Model:			
				1	2	5	6
U	0	0	196	101.3	138.7	196.4	196.0
q		1	45	45.6	62.4	41.5	43.9
		2+	10	36.5	49.9	13.1	12.2
	1–2	0	52	50.6	44.8	49.8	48.5
		1	21	22.8	20.1	22.2	19.1
		2+	8	18.2	16.1	9.1	9.3
	3+	0	13	50.3	18.8	14.8	16.1
		1	8	22.6	8.4	10.4	11.2
		2+	13	18.1	6.8	8.8	9.6
N	0	0	140	112.1	111.6	140.8	139.8
		1	39	50.4	50.2	42.2	44.6
		2+	23	40.4	40.2	19.0	17.6
	1–2	0	51	56.0	58.0	52.5	55.5
		1	35	25.2	26.1	33.2	31.2
		2+	19	20.2	20.9	19.3	21.7
	3+	0	33	55.6	54.1	30.7	29.6
		1	32	25.0	24.4	30.5	29.2
		2+	33	20.0	19.5	36.8	35.7
F	0	0	55	87.2	50.3	53.8	52.5
		1	22	39.2	22.6	22.3	23.9
		2+	14	31.4	18.1	14.9	13.4
	1–2	0	32	43.6	47.5	32.7	33.4
		1	28	19.6	21.4	28.6	26.7
		2+	26	15.7	17.1	24.7	26.5
	3+	0	28	43.3	76.2	28.5	28.5
		1	40	19.5	34.3	39.1	40.1
		2+	70	15.6	27.5	70.4	69.9

NOTE: The models are: (1) Independence [(A) (F) (L)]
(2) Conditional Independence [(FL) (A)]
(5) Pairwise Association [(AF) (AL) (FL)]
(6) Pairwise Uniform Association

The variables are: (A) Delinquent Acts
(F) Delinquent Friends
(L) Attitude Toward Breaking the Law

where i, j, nd k are index acts, friends, and definitions, respectively.
Parameterization of this model is shown in Table 6.9. Each entry shows
b_{FA}, b_{FL}, or b_{AL} multiplied by the appropriate row-column product:
$(i-1)(j-1)$, $(i-1)(k-1)$, and $(j-1)(k-1)$, respectively.

The pairwise uniform association model (M6) fits very well ($L^2 = 8.49$;
df = 17; p > .50). The three parameters, $b_{FA} = .56, b_{FL} = .35$, and $b_{AL} = .47$,

TABLE 6.7 Goodness of Fit for Selected Models of Delinquent Acts (A) by Delinquent Friends (F) by Attitude Toward Breaking the Law (L)

Model	L^2	df	P	L^2_m/L^2_1
1. (A) (F) (L)	370.37	20	<.001	1.000
2. (FL) (A)	228.45	16	<.001	.617
3. (FL) (A)	44.45	12	<.001	.120
4. (FL) (AL)	124.51	12	<.001	.336
5. (FL) (AF) (AL)	6.01	8	>.50	.016
6. Pairwise Uniform Association	8.49	17	>.50	.023
(1) - (2)	141.92	4	<.001	
(2) - (3)	184.00	4	<.001	
(2) - (4)	103.94	4	<.001	
(3) - (5)	38.44	4	<.001	
(4) - (5)	118.50	4	<.001	
(1) - (6)	361.88	3	<.001	
(6) - (5)	2.48	9	>.50	

account for all but a trivial 2.3 percent of the association in the table. The relationship of delinquency to friends and definitions conducive to breaking the law are graphed in Figure 6.2. The log-odds on one delinquent act (relative to none) and on two or more (relative to one) increase linearly with the number of delinquent friends for youths with each type of definition. The slope of each line is .56; that is, the log-odds on delinquent behavior are greater by .56 units for youths with one or two delinquent friends than for youths with no delinquent friends. Another increment of .56 units in the log-odds on delinquent behavior follows an increase from one or two to three or more delinquent friends. The line for youths with unfavorable definitions is at the bottom of the graph. The line for youths with neutral definitions lies .35 units above the bottom line, and the line for youths whose definitions favor breaking the law lies .35 units above the line for neutrals.

As in the bivariate analysis, the analogy between the UA parameters and regression coefficients is compelling. The regression coefficient is the slope of the line relating values of the independent variable to expected values of the dependent variable. The UA parameter is the slope of the line relating values of the independent variable to expected odds on values of the dependent variable. But as I pointed out before, the UA model contains a built-in stochastic component that allows it to predict the entire

TABLE 6.8 Parameter Estimates of Model 5 (Pairwise Association)

Effect		Index	Level 1	Level 2	Level 3
Grand Mean			3.39		
Marginals:	A	i	.50	−.06	−.44
	F	j	.27	−.10	−.18
	L	k	−.28	.22	.06
Two-Way	AF	1j	.57	−.08	−.49
		2j	−.01	.09	−.08
		3j	−.56	−.01	.57
	AL	1k	.35	.01	−.36
		2k	.00	.01	−.01
		3k	−.35	−.02	.37
	FL	1k	.48	−.01	−.47
		2K	.05	−.04	−.01
		3K	−.53	.05	.48

TABLE 6.9 Parameterization of Pairwise Uniform Association Model

Law	Friends	(AF) Association Acts 0	1	2+	(AL) Association Acts 0	1	2+	(FL) Association Acts 0	1	2+
Unfavorable	0									
	1–2		a	2a						
	3+		2a	4a						
Neutral	0					b	2b			
	1–2		a	2a		b	2b	c	c	c
	3+		2a	4a		b	2b	2c	2c	2c
Favorable	0					2b	4b			
	1–2		a	2a		2b	4b	2c	2c	2c
	3+		2a	4a		2b	4b	4c	4c	4c

distribution of the dependent variable for given values of the independent variable.

PROGRAMS FOR THE UA MODEL

The parameter estimates and expected frequencies reported in this chapter were obtained using Haberman's (1979: 571-585) program,

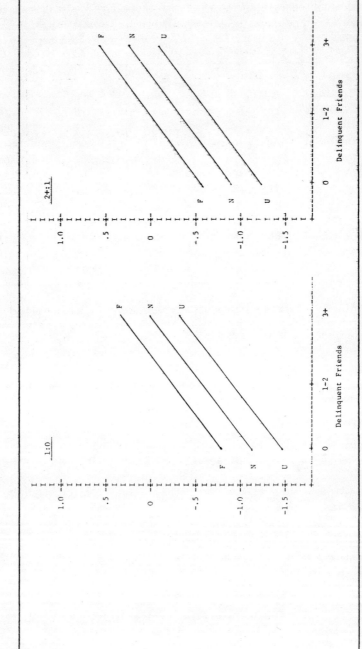

Figure 6.2 Log-Odds on Delinquency Expected Under Uniform Association by Friends Within Categories of Attitude Toward the Law

FREQ. The program employs a Newton-Raphson method for obtaining maximum-likelihood estimates. The parameterizations shown in Tables 6.3 and 6.9, along with sets of dummy variables for the marginal effects, will produce the results reported in the text and tables. Goodman (1979a) describes an algorithm that also produces maximum-likelihood estimates.

CONCLUSION

This chapter has uncovered a very simple structure to the three-way cross-classification of delinquent behavior, friends, and definitions presented by Jensen (1972). The associations among the three variables are uniform, linear, and additive. Three parametes capture 98 percent of the association in the 27 cells of the three-way table.

The pairwise uniform association model is superior to the standard proportion reduction in error (PRE) measures usually calculated for Table 6.6 because the UA parameters are independent of marginal shifts and interpretable in terms of causal process rather than prediction accuracy. The PRE measures tell how much knowledge of the joint distribution improves the researcher's ability to make predictions about the dependent variable relative to the accuracy obtained using just the marginal distribution. For ordered tables, the PRE measure for ordered tables, gamma, measures improvement in predicting order for pairs of cases, not outcomes on the dependent variable. The UA parameter, on the other hand, has a rather simple interpretation that is causal rather than predictive. The UA parameter is the amount of increase or decrease in the odds on a given outcome to be expected from a shift of one unit in the independent variable.

The UA model also has an advantage over the general log-linear model. The UA model is more parsimonious. To fit pairwise association in the general log-linear model requires $(A-1)(B-1)$ degrees of freedom, A and B being the number of categories in the two variables under consideration for each two-way association fitted. The UA model fits a single parameter (one degree of freedom) to each two-way association. In that sense it is a very powerful model. The UA model can detect a small but significant association that might be missed by the general log-linear model if that association is linear and additive and the categories are equally spaced. On the other hand, if any of the assumptions of the model are violated, the UA model will not fit the data. That, too, is important information.

REFERENCES

CLOGG, C. C. (forthcoming) "Using association models in sociological research: some examples." Amer. J. of Sociology.

DUNCAN, O. D. (1979) "How destination depends on origin in the mobility table." Amer. J. of Sociology 84: 793-804.

FIENBERG, S. E. (1980) The Analysis of Cross-Classified Categorical Data. Cambridge: MIT Press.

GOODMAN, L. A. (1979a) "Simple models for the analysis of doubly ordered cross-classifications." J. of the Amer. Statistical Assoc. 74: 537-552.

——— (1979b) "Multiplicative models for the mobility table." Amer. J. of Sociology 84: 804-819.

——— (1972) "A general model for the analysis of surveys." Amer. J. of Sociology 77: 1035-1086.

——— (1970) "The multivariate analysis of qualitative data: interactions among multiple classifications." J. of the Amer. Statistical Assoc. 65: 226-56.

——— (1969) "How to ransack mobility tables and other cross-classifications having ordered rows and columns." Amer. J. of Sociology 75: 1-35.

HABERMAN, S. J. (1979) The Analysis of Qualitative Data, Vol. 2. New York: Academic Press.

——— (1974) "Log-linear models for frequency tables with ordered classifications." Biometrics 30: 589-600.

JENSEN, G. F. (1972) "Parents, peers, and delinquent action: a test of the differential association perspective." Amer. J. of Sociology 78: 562-575.

7

Alan J. Lizotte
Indiana University

James Mercy
Emory University

Eric Monkkonen
University of California, Los Angeles

CRIME AND POLICE STRENGTH
IN AN URBAN SETTING
Chicago, 1947-1970

The untangling of the relationships between the urban social and economic structure, the funding and behavior of police, and criminal behavior continues to be a major analytic challenge to social scientists. Within the broad set of issues, a key theoretical decision concerns the inclusion or exclusion of variables indexing power, its differential diffusion, and the consequences of this diffusion. The primary question is, "Does power inequality have direct effects on the behavior of police and on the behavior of criminal offenders?" If a society has power inequality but is also just, this inequality should not affect the behavior of the police; nor, if all members of the society share the same conception of actual justness, should this inequality affect the criminal behavior of individuals or groups with differential access to power. On the other hand, if a society has both power inequality and only partial justness, then the power inequality may be reflected in the behavior of both crime control agents and crime producers.

AUTHORS' NOTE: We are indebted to David Greenberg, Larry Griffin, Colin Loftin, Cynthia Rexroat, Douglas A. Smith, and Faith Wolfson for helpful comments on earlier drafts of this chapter.

Sometimes, but not always, those social scientists who identify themselves as conflict theorists operate from the theoretical perspective entailed
by the second position, while those identified as consensus theorists
operate from the perspective entailed by the first position. Disagreements
occur at two points, not just one, for while the first question concerns the
inclusion of power inequality indicators at all in any model specification,
the second concerns the conceptual basis for measuring power inequality.
Most commonly, income inequality serves as the indicator for power
inequality for rather obvious, though not necessarily good, reasons: Wealth
is both a source of power and a reward for the exercise of power. (Never
mind that Robert Moses, called the "power broker" by Caro, was not
wealthy or that income may not accurately index wealth.) The conceptual
difficulty with this measure of inequality arises from the same elements as
does its appeal. Although on the individual and personal level income
inequality seems to be socially significant, from the perspective of the
social structure, income inequality is a phenomenon which may be only an
incidental byproduct of the inequality of the distribution of power.
(Additionally, in an important sense, by using income inequality as an
indicator we use the effect and not the cause.)

A more appropriate concept for measuring power inequality in a
capitalist society is Marx's notion of the rate of surplus value, which, as
defined, measures the power of capital over the power of labor. The
greater the rate of surplus value that can be extracted from labor, the
greater the power of capital. Although the concept of the rate of surplus
value has clear theoretical relevance to the notion of power inequality, the
actual indexing of the rate of surplus value is less straightforward (see
"Data and Methods," below). Thus, in comparison to income inequality,
the straightforward concept of the rate of surplus value must be crudely
operationalized, while the income inequality measure quite tidily opera-
tionalizes a concept unclearly embedded in theory (Williamson and
Lindert, 1981). In this chapter we have chosen to operationalize the rate
of surplus value as the dollar value added by manufacture, divided by
wages to production workers—that is, the value added by the manufacturing process net of labor costs. While recognizing the crudeness of this
measure, we feel that it represents a more adequate definition of power
distribution than any income inequality measure due to its theoretical
grounding.

When the question addresses police funding and behavior relative to
powerless social groups, a measure of power, not wealth or income, is the
most appropriate beginning. After all, in a relatively democratic society, to
take wealth or income as the sole index of power is to deny the very real,
if limited, political power of the economically disadvantaged. In the
remainder of our argument for estimating the model which follows, we

stress the notion of conceptually relevant variables, for our larger purpose here is to contribute to research grounded in both theory and reasonable operationalizations of theory.

Several principles determine the models estimated here. First, any analysis of the forces that determine police per capita should consider the interrelations among determinants of police strength, police expenditures, and crime (McPheters and Stronge, 1976). As Jacobs (1979) has shown, crime may partly determine police strength, but simultaneously police strength may also affect the crime rate. Snyder and Tilly (1972: 526) explain: "High levels of governmental repression . . . increase the costs of collective action. They thereby decrease the likelihood that groups will mobilize and make claims which are unacceptable to existing members of the polity. Repression thus reduces the extent of collective violence." The same logic holds for government repression and crime. Economic factors determine the city's revenues in one year, which in turn fix police expenditures and the actual number of police in the next year. In turn, this level of police strength affects the crime rate in a third year.

Clearly, this system of relations in time must be studied to capture the complicated direct and indirect effects economic power may have on police strength. A parsimonious analysis would consider one aggregate unit over time—preferably, one city. Larger aggregates cloud the dynamic picture, unless the focus of the analysis is parallel structural development. The focus on one city solves problems inherent in other approaches by making the unit of comparison more homogeneous. Often, cross-sectional analyses of cities beg the question of where a particular city falls in the historical continuum of change. In fact, such studies assume progressive change (big more developed than small) or stasis (all developmentally similar). A time series on one city accounts for this naturally.

Often, sociological studies ignore the tax base of cities as a determinant of police strength. Yet it should be obvious that the ability to raise revenue is an important determinant of police expenditures (see Weicher, 1976; McPheters and Stronge, 1976). Since most police expenditure dollars pay operating costs rather than capital costs (Bordua and Haurek, 1970), these expenditures control the number of police officers per capita. Because a city's ability to raise revenues probably relates to its economic inequality, any relation between economic inequality and police strength must be placed in the context of the tax base.

Finally, inadequate measurement of the economic power of the black community can render findings from both the consensus and conflict perspectives spurious. For example, two plausible reasons exist which account for the size of the black population in a city affecting police strength. First, this relation could indicate racism rather than economic motivation. Since conflict theory locates the demand for police strength in the realm of economic power, the relationship in this case would reject conflict theory in fact but not in appearance. Second, the black-police strength relation as measured could be spurious, deriving from a poor measurement of power. Black population size could fail to predict police strength simply because the measures of income inequality do not reflect the power of the lower classes.

The research reported here addresses both the theoretical and the empirical issues related to the effects of race and economic factors on crime and police strength using data from 1947 to 1970 for the city of Chicago. The following section will elaborate a parsimonious model and test of the conflict and consensus models with regard to surplus value, crime, and police strength.

DATA AND METHODS

This study uses data from 1947 to 1970 for the city of Chicago. Many of the data were acquired from *Chicago Since 1840: A Time Series Handbook* (see Skogan, 1976), supplemented with data from the *Uniform Crime Reports* and the *Census of Manufacturers.*

Ordinary least squares is used to estimate a five-equation macrodynamic structural equation model of surplus value, property crime, violent crime, police expenditures, and police per capita. Relations which were insignificant at the .1 level were excluded from the analysis, and equations were then reestimated.

Table 7.1 displays the variable codes, with variable names listed in the lefthand portion of the table and descriptions of those variables in the right.[1] For example, the table shows that Popcops is the number of police department personnel per capita. The coding of most variables is straightforward. Therefore, only the coding of surplus value will be discussed.

Since this research is "concerned specifically with the relations of social classes in class-based society" (Applebaum, 1978: 73), the rate of surplus value is used to measure the economic power of the capitalist class. The rate of surplus value indexes "an exact expression for the degree of exploitation of labour-power by capital, or the labourer by the capitalist" (Marx, 1906: 241).

> Surplus value is explained by reference to the fact that, as the labour-power of the worker is a commodity, its "cost of production" can be calculated just like any other commodity. This is constituted by the cost of providing the worker with sufficient returns to "Produce and reproduce himself": the differential between this and the total value created by the worker is the source of surplus value [Giddens, 1973: 34].

TABLE 7.1   Description of Variables Used in the Analysis

Variable Name	Description of Variable
Popcops	Total number of police department personnel per capita; $\overline{X}$ = .003 s.d. = .0007
PolExp	Constant dollar police expenditures per capita; $\overline{X}$ = 19.5 s.d. = 15.5
Property Crime	Number of reported burglaries, larcenies over $50, and auto thefts per capita; $\overline{X}$ = .015 s.d. = .009
Violent Crime	Number of reported murders, robberies, and assaults per capita; $\overline{X}$ = .006 s.d. = .003
Rate of Surplus Value	Value of shipments in manufacturing − wages of production workers − cost of materials / wages of production workers; $\overline{X}$ = 1.882 s.d. = .2522
Exogenous Variables	
Tax	General revenues in the corporate fund for the city in constant dollars per capita; $\overline{X}$ = 464.65 s.d. 307.45
%Professional	Percentage of the city population in professional occupations; $\overline{X}$ = 9.53 s.d. = 1.22
Average Firm Size	Average firm size = total number of wage workers in manufacturing / number of manufacturing establishments; $\overline{X}$ = 59.7 s.d. = 3.8
% Black	$\overline{X}$ = 21.16 s.d. = 6.76
Traffic Citations	Number of traffic citations and arrests per capita; $\overline{X}$ = .402 s.d. = .226
Manufacturing	Number of manufacturing establishments; $\overline{X}$ = 9611 s.d. = 729
% Under 21	Percentage of population under 21 years of age; $\overline{X}$ = 32.9 s.d. = 3.5
Business Failures	Rate of business failures in the U.S.; $\overline{X}$ = .421 s.d. = .150
Unemployment	U.S. unemployment rate; $\overline{X}$ = 4.63 s.d. = 1.12

Specifically, for any individual firm surplus value (S) is the sum of profit, interest, and rent. In Marx's notation the *rate* of surplus value is

$$\text{rate of surplus value} = \frac{S}{V} \qquad [1]$$

where V refers to variable capital (see for example Klein, 1968: 155). "Variable capital refers to capital reserved for payment of wages, and is so called because it is the category which is considered to be the source of all new value created and thus finds its raison d'être only if it is variable" (Tsuru, 1968: 180). V only includes wages of those workers responsible for creating value in the production process. Excluded from V are wages to workers who are involved in activities such as advertising. Their labor is used only to create artificial demand for goods that already have value.

"Most Marxists, therefore, in their practical calculations . . . [use] the 'real rate of surplus value,' to denote the division of value added over a year" (Kühne, 1979: 111). That is, for practical purposes the rate of surplus value in a manufacturing firm is equal to value added to manufacturing minus wages of production workers all divided by wages of production workers. Of course, this calculation ignores the interest and rent components of surplus value. But this violation is not great if the researcher is interested in the rate of exploitation in the creation of value in the production process alone.

Aggregation of rates of surplus value over firms is not problematic. Using an identical measure, Amsden (1981) aggregated rates of surplus value in manufacturing for nations. Similarly, Baran and Sweezy (1966) aggregated surplus value for the period 1929 to 1963 for the United States. There are severe problems related to aggregating Marx's rate of profit or the organic composition of capital over firms. This is because aggregation assumes that constant capital (C) in equation 2 is equal across firms when clearly it is not (see for example Morishima, 1973: 87-104).

$$\text{rate of profit} = \frac{S}{C + V} \qquad [2]$$

Since this research is concerned with how the rate of exploitation of labor relates to crime and police strength, the rate of profit and the aggregation problem are of no significance.

In essence, the rate of surplus value is profit to capital divided by wages to production labor. In this analysis the rate of surplus value is computed only for manufacturing establishments, for two reasons. First, the data are readily available for manufacturing. As American census enumerators began to record "dollar value added by manufacture," at the same time in the nineteenth century Marx reconceptualized the same figure as surplus value. Second, the rate of surplus value in manufacturing indexes the working class-capitalist class power relationship, whereas the rate of surplus value in white-collar industry (i.e., insurance, banking) would tap the middle class-capitalist class power differential.

One might object to the aggregation of the rate of surplus value in manufacturing because some firms in Chicago are multinational. Hence, part of the surplus would be disposed of in places other than Chicago. Despite this, it is still true that regardless of where the surplus is spent, Chicago's workers create it. The surplus value accumulated is due to their labor, and capitalists are more or less powerful because of that labor.

Regardless of where surplus value goes, the rate of exploitation or the rate of surplus value can be calculated for workers in Chicago. If the labor theory of value is correct, high rates of exploitation should generate high rates of property crime. In this case workers could close the gap in exploitation by turning to crime. Additionally, as Marx points out, the police in capitalistic society are in part a tool to protect the accumulation of surplus value (Marx, 1968: 26). So police strength should respond positively to the rate of surplus value.

For the period 1947 to 1970 the average rate of surplus value in Chicago's manufacturing industry was 192 percent. The 1970 figure was 229 percent. Amsden (1981) found that for 1969 to 1977 the average rate of surplus value in total U.S. manufacturing industry was 249 percent. Since the rate of surplus value increases over time, there is remarkable similarity between Chicago's rate of surplus value and the nation's rate as calculated by Amsden (1981), if the different levels of aggregation and the slightly different time periods are considered.

ANALYSIS AND RESULTS

Figure 7.1 shows the final estimated path model predicting surplus value, crime, and police strength. Insignificant paths have been dropped from the model.[2] Standardized coefficients are used to compare effects. Table 7.2 displays unstandardized coefficients with standard errors in parentheses. The equations show no sign of autocorrelation using Durbin's H (Durbin, 1970) when lagged endogenous effects are present, or the standard Durbin-Watson statistic when no lagged endogenous effects occur. Further, comparison of the explained variance (R^2) for equations with the adjusted R^2s show strong time-dependent equilibrating processes (see Land and Felson, 1976: 590). In general, the six equations provide a very good fit of the data. Explained variance ranges from a low of 94.6 percent (property crime) to a high of 99.9 percent (police expenditures). Lagged endogenous variables have been included in most equations. This "detrends" endogenous variables, reduces autocorrelation, adds a dynamic structure to the equations, and provides theoretical insight.

Figure 7.1 provides a heuristic device that will be helpful in interpreting equations in terms of power inequality. Before discussing relations in the model it is important to point out that the high correlation between percentage black and surplus value (.967) necessitates a choice between one variable or the other for any particular equation. In essence, when both are included in the same equation, they cancel each other. This has interesting theoretical implications. It suggests that the expropriation of surplus value is closely tied to the maintenance of a low wage, minority,

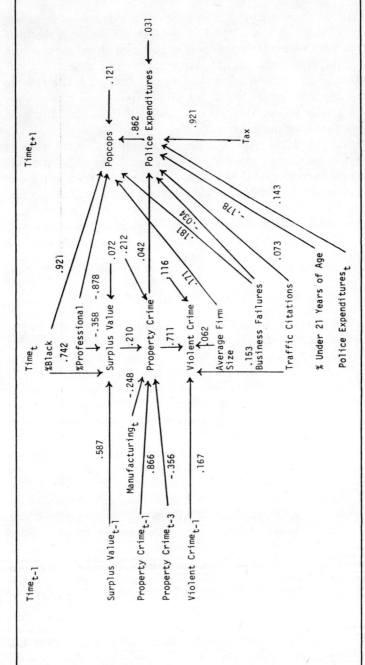

Figure 7.1 A Five-Equation Model of Surplus Value, Property Crime, Police Expenditures, and Police per Capita

NOTE: Standardized ordinary least squares regression coefficients are used to measure effects.

peripheral labor force. Amsden (1981: 236-237) lends support to this interpretation: "The extraordinarily high rates of surplus value in countries which are now described as semi-industrialised may be hypothesised to stem from a combination of advanced technology and wage levels that are still abysmal." In part, this is because workers in semiindustrialized countries, like workers in the U.S. periphery, for a variety of reasons lack bargaining strength. As such, theoretical concerns would dictate choosing surplus value over percentage black when they cancel each other. A more conservative approach is used here. For any given equation, the variable that contributes most to the explained variance is used.[3]

In general, the equations in Table 7.2 and Figure 7.1 show that economic power plays an important role in determining crime rates and police strength. The number of police per capita is a function of business failures, average firm size, percentage black, percentage professional, and police expenditures. When business failures increase, this police department chooses to allocate more resources to personnel. Of course, an increase in business failures means economic hard times. This economic turmoil could lead to increases in crime. The police respond with increased manpower to deter the possible increase in the crime rate.

In large part, the budget determines the strength of a police department. Bordua and Haurek (1970) estimate that wages and salaries account for 90 percent of public expenditures for police, a proportion that appears to have been relatively constant from the turn of the century until 1960. Because of the labor-intensive nature of policing, the manpower allocated to a police department indicates police strength. Correspondingly, police per capita is strongly related to police expenditures, just as the amount of tax revenues is a powerful determinant of police expenditures.

In any realm of public activity, budgeting translates financial resources into policy. The budget lies at the heart of the political process, reflecting the outcome of a more complex struggle (Wildavsky, 1974: 1-5). "In a market economy, fiscal expenditures are excellent indicators of the process of societal resource allocation" (Bordua and Haurek, 1970: 58). Politicians, interest groups, and individual citizens vie with one another to influence how the budget will be allocated.

Blauner (1970: 177) suggests that in some large firms "social control rests less on consensus and more on the power of management to enforce compliance to the rule system of the factory." Workers in large firms lean toward "occasional militant action" (1970: 178) with which police must deal. Interestingly, as firms in Chicago become larger and more powerful, they seem to influence the allocation of the police budget—that is, they demand that more public resources be spent on police personnel in order to protect their expanded capital investment.[4]

TABLE 7.2 Equations Predicting Surplus Value, Property Crime, Violent Crime, Police Expenditures, and Police Per Capita

Variables	Surplus Value	Property Crime	Violent Crime	Pol Exp	PopCops
Surplus Value$_{t-1}$	.54515 (.06943)				
%Black$_t$	.00003 (.00000)				.00010 (.00002)
%Professional$_t$	−.00007 (.00001)				−.00052 (.00013)
Manufacturing$_t$		−.00000 (.00000)			
Surplus Value$_t$		7,18635 (3.56242)			
Property Crime$_{t-1}$		.89373 (.11973)			
Property Crime$_{t-3}$		−.38502 (.12001)			
Property Crime$_t$			.24383 (.02574)	75.56192 (29.28469)	
Violent Crime$_{t-1}$			.17539 (.09124)		
Firm Size$_t$			.00005 (.00002)		.00003 (.00002)

Traffic$_t$			.00200 (.00079)	4.99923 (2.13861)	
% Under 21$_t$				-.80064 (.12721)	
Tax$_{t+1}$				.04655 (.00354)	
Business Failures$_t$				3.522151 (1.20102)	.00087 (.00040)
Pol Exp$_{t+1 \text{ or } t}$				.18175 (.09838)	.00004 (.00001)
Intercept	.00145	.01464	-.00297	19.44341	.00272
R^2	.9948	.9551	.9864	.9995	.9853
Adjusted R^2	.9940	.9456	.9836	.9993	.9812
Durbin-Watson or Durbin's H	1.0904	.9812	.0981	2.43623	

NOTE: Unstandardized coefficients are reported; standard errors are in parentheses.

When the city population contains a high percentage of professionals, police per capita will be low. In other words, the larger the proportion of white-collar professional workers in the city, the less is the perceived need for intensive policing. Additionally, as one would expect from previous research (see Loftin et al., 1981; and Jacobs, 1979), as the percentage of blacks in the city increases, police per capita increases independent of the crime rate. In other words, the black population size determines police strength independent of the amount of crime which that population produces.

Not too surprisingly, the amount of money allocated to the police is largely a function of the amount of money available to the city. Independent of this, increases in business failures mean a weak business sector. This translates into lower police funding. In essence, the number of police and police expenditures are enhanced when business is relatively powerful, and they are cut when business is weak.

Independent of the tax base, police departments can generate some revenues for the city through traffic citations. Increased vigilance in issuing traffic citations and making traffic arrests increases tax revenues, and, indirectly, the police budget. Thus, there may be budgetary incentives for police departments to fight traffic and not crime.

Increases in the property crime rate translate into enhanced police funding. Additionally, a large young population probably indicates a weak tax base and therefore lower police funding. Finally, police expenditures in one year predict expenditures in the next, reflecting organizational "inertia" and the positive trend in the funding of police from year to year.

In general, the enforcement side of the model indicates that economic power plays an important role in determining police strength. Average firm size, business failures, and weak minority populations all predict police strength.

Economic power also plays an important role in determining crime rates. Police expenditures and police per capita do not influence the crime rates. Rather, average firm size, traffic citations and arrests, the property crime rate, and the violent crime rate lagged one year all predict the rate of violent crime.

Average firm size is a good predictor of the violent crime rate in a city. Blauner (1970: 178) argues that the personality of a worker in some large firms "is expressed in a characteristic attitude of cynicism toward authority and institutional systems, and a volatility revealed in aggressive responses to infringements on personal rights and occasional militant collective action." In other words, as firms in the industrial sector become large, workers become more alienated and more aggressive. This alienation results in an elevated violent crime rate.

The violent crime rate is probably related to the property crime rate for two reasons. First, some property crimes inadvertently become violent crimes. For example, a burglar inadvertently encountering and striking a homeowner converts an initial property crime into a violent crime. Second, some criminals may commit both types of crime (Land and Felson, 1976: 592). Therefore, the relation between property crime and violent crime measures the involvement of some persons in both types of crime and the propensity of property crime to translate into violent crime.

Traffic citations have an interesting effect, for as the police become more vigilant in issuing traffic citations and making traffic arrests, violent crime increases. There could be a variety of reasons for this phenomenon. First, it could be due to the allocation of finite resources from crime control to traffic control. That is, a police department has a fixed level of resources: the more time police spend on traffic control, the less time they can spend on detecting and deterring crime. This interpretation seems weak, since officers placed on traffic assignments are not likely to be drawn from actual crime-fighting units. Typically, they would be assigned from more mundane jobs. Second, issuing traffic citations exposes the police to a broad spectrum of the adult population, perhaps encouraging people to report crimes to the police. That is, this relation could be the result of increased reporting due to increased police exposure. Third, the effect of traffic citations and arrests on the violent crime rate could be the result of increased crime detection during traffic control. In other words, the police might discover some crimes during the process of issuing traffic citations—at least they expect to do so (Reiss, 1971). This is probably the strongest interpretation of this finding. Most violence in police-citizen encounters occurs in marginal (initially not serious) offenses, where citizens feel the police have been too arbitrary. Hence, increases in traffic citations may generate violent crime. Moreover, "traffic stops" have a traditional method of finding offenders and detecting offenses (Rubenstein, 1973).

Importantly, the percentage of the population that is black relates to neither violent nor property crime. In fact, property crime responds only to lagged endogenous effects, the number of manufacturing establishments, and surplus value. As with violent crime, there is a positive trend in property crime. The effect of property crime at time t-1 on property crime at time t suggests general increases in the number of people at risk to commit property crime. Additionally, property crime lagged three years has a negative effect on property crime. This suggests that over time property crime tracks as a monotonically increasing function with oscillations at about three-year intervals.[5]

In addition to this trend in the property crime rate, as the number of manufacturing establishments increases, the property crime rate decreases. Similarly, Lane (1979) demonstrates that the growth of the large-scale, industrial work place in nineteenth-century Philadelphia tamed interpersonal violence and internalized individual conflict.

Conversely, as surplus value increases, property crime also increases. This suggests that the relative economic hardship embodied in surplus value directly generates economic crime and indirectly generates violent crime. Additionally, property crime is insensitive to the relative size of the black population independent of the economic posture of the black community. That is, the economic exploitation embodied in the rate of surplus value accounts for blacks' propensity to commit property crime.

Finally, the rate of surplus value produced in a year is a function of the type of labor force within the city. Blacks comprise a low-wage, labor-intensive, peripheral labor force due to their exclusion from core sector jobs. As such, blacks provide a cheap, easily expendable labor pool which can be tapped at will, providing an opportunity for capital to generate high profits relative to labor's share of revenue. Alternatively, a high proportion of professionals indicates a healthy core sector labor force which is highly trained, expensive, and not easily expendable. Here profits to capital are low relative to wages of professional workers. This is one reason why the state must subsidize their training. Therefore, increases in the professional labor force decrease the amount of surplus value expropriated by capital. Of course, there is a positive trend over time in the rate of surplus value generated by Chicago's manufacturing industry.

Table 7.3 shows that excluding surplus value from the property crime equation results in percentage black becoming a significant predictor. Again, this suggests that the familiar finding that blacks are heavily involved in crime can be subsumed under the rubric of exploitation as indicated by surplus value. Similarly, if percentage black is excluded from the police per capita equation, surplus value becomes a significant predictor.

Forecasting is one method which can be used to evaluate the adequacy of a time series model (see Land and Felson, 1976; Christ, 1966). Because the *Uniform Crime Reports* use a new definition for larceny beginning in 1973, forecasting is not possible after 1972. The police per capita and police expenditure equations were estimated for 1947 to 1970. This means that forecasts are possible for 1971 and 1972 for those equations. The crime and surplus value equations were estimated for the period 1946 to 1969. Therefore, three years of forecasts are possible (1971, 1972, 1973). Table 7.4 shows two- and three-year forecasts for the five equations. With one exception, the forecasts are relatively accurate. Both crime equations, the surplus value equation, and the police per capita equation all forecast very accurately one year into the future, with accuracy falling marginally at the second-year forecast. Therefore observations subsequent to estimation seem to be generated by the causal structure of the period used to

TABLE 7.3   Property Crime Equation with Percentage Black Included and Surplus Value Excluded, and Police Per Capita Equation with Surplus Value Included and Percentage Black Excluded

Variables	Property Crime	Police Per Capita
Property Crime$_{t-1}$	.9234 (.1190)	
Property Crime$_{t-3}$	-.4112 (.1231)	
Manufacturing	-.0000 (.0000)	
%Black	.0004 (.0002)	
Surplus Value		1.1440 (.5466)
Police Expenditures		.00004 (.00001)
Avarage Firm Size		.00001 (.00002)
Business Failures		.0007 (.0005)
%Professional		-.0002 (.0001)
Intercept	.0169	-.0001
R^2	.953	.977
Adjusted R^2	.943	.971
Durbin-Watson or Durbin's H	1.08588	1.99088

NOTE: Unstandardized coefficients are reported; standard errors are in parentheses.

estimate the equations. However, the police expenditure equation does not forecast well. In this equation forecasts are consistently higher than observed values. This is probably because of dramatic changes in police funding at the end of the estimation period. Inspection of the police expenditure data shows that police expenditures increased dramatically in 1968 and 1969, then began declining back to a normal level in 1970, 1971, and 1972. This dramatic increase probably occurred for two reasons. First, the Democratic National Convention was held in Chicago in 1968. Rioting was expected, and the police planned to be ready. Their funding was increased substantially. Second, in 1968 Martin Luther King

TABLE 7.4   Conditional Forecasts of the 1971, 1972, and 1973 Values for the Five Equations

Year	Observed	Forecast	Error	Standard Error of the Estimate	# of Standard Errors Off
Property Crime					
1970	.0270	.02989	−.00289	.00201	1.44
1971	.0267	.03053	−.00383	.00201	1.91
1972	.0255	.03017	−.00471	.00201	2.34
Violent Crime					
1970	.0106	.01040	.00020	.00038	.53
1971	.0108	.01038	.00042	.00038	1.11
1972	.0106	.01009	−.00054	.00038	1.43
Surplus Value					
1970	2.238	2.2224	.0156	.02000	.78
1971	2.266	2.2472	.0188	.02000	.94
1972	2.293	2.2675	.0255	.02000	1.28
Police Per Capita					
1971	.0050	.004987	.0000129	.00010	.13
1972	.0051	.005177	−.000077	.00010	.77
Police Expenditures					
1971	75.9894	81.3565	−5.3716	.40126	13.39
1972	82.5022	85.0784	−2.5762	.40126	6.42

died. Rioting engulfed the city, leaving nine dead and many injured, with extensive looting and property damage. This riot, like the police riot, had the effect of increasing police expenditures. The data suggest that more trouble was expected in 1969 and police funding was kept high. Since this massive structural change in funding occurred at the end of the period of estimation, with only a hint of a return to normal in 1970, the equation predicts much higher levels of police funding than actually occurred. By 1972 the prediction is much better, but still not within two standard errors of the estimate of the equation.

Equation 3 compares the root mean square error of the two-year forecast ($RMSE_F$) to that of the "naive" model of no change in the dependent variable from one year to the next ($RMSE_N$; see Christ, 1966).

This calculation suggests that the police expenditure equation forecasts twice as well as the no-change model.

$$\frac{RMSE_f}{RMSE_n} = .50 \qquad [3]$$

Hence, the police expenditure equation predicts better than the no-change model, but it is not wholly adequate. This poor prediction is probably due to dramatic structural change in police funding in 1968 and 1969.

CONCLUSION

These data lend plausibility to a model which measures economic power as the rate of surplus value. Other indicators of the power of capital relative to labor also were found to exert an influence on police strength, for the size of manufacturing establishments and business failures combined to dictate police strength. These influences of capital on police strength acted independently of the incidence of crime. Moreover, police strength has no influence on crime rates independent of economic power.

Despite the ease with which an index of the rate of surplus value can be calculated, criminologists and sociologists have largely ignored it in empirical investigations. Yet, this analysis shows that the rate of surplus value accounts for all of the relationship between percentage black and crime. In other words, the pervasive research findings that blacks are disproportionately likely to be involved in crime can be accounted for by the relative powerlessness of blacks in our capitalistic society. This conclusion challenges contemporary notions that the inadequate socialization (or deterioration) of black families, or a black subculture itself, explains differential black crime rates. The reasons lie in the structure of power, not in the family.

At first glance, the rate of surplus value seems to play an important role in determining crime rates. But in order to evaluate its significance fully, future research should test surplus value's effect using cross-sectional data and data on other periods. For example, one would expect that the rate of surplus value could also explain the effects of percentage Italian on crime in the 1930s and '40s, just as it should explain the effect of percentage Irish on pre-World War I crime. Such findings would not be surprising in light of the classic work of Shaw and McKay (1942), who found that areas, not populations, maintained crime rates over time. In particular, they found that areas with high crime were deteriorated areas, where industry had encroached on the community. One minority population after another inhabited these deteriorated neighborhoods, exhibiting high crime rates while living in these impoverished neighborhoods. It is a short journey, via dual labor market theory, to argue that the structural inequality of power endemic to capitalism, and hence the rate of surplus value, lies at the root of crime in these populations and neighborhoods. Independent of the power of industry and surplus value expropriated, the police do not become differentially powerful when there is a large black population. The police are not powerful for racism's sake, but for capital's sake.

NOTES

1. A number of variables used in this analysis required that midpanel interpolation techniques be used to estimate missing values. Data for the percentage black and percentage under 21 were available for decadal census years in the city of Chicago. Therefore, the Karup-King third-difference formula was used to estimate data points between census years for the period 1940 to 1970. This formula is an oscillatory interpolation equation based on overlapping polynomials of the second degree (Shyrock and Siegal, 1975: 688). The equation for the formula is as follows:

$$Y_{n+1+x} = Y_n + \frac{(x+1)}{1!} \Delta Y_n + \frac{(x+1)x}{2!} \Delta^2 Y_n + \frac{x^2(x+1)}{3!} \Delta^3 Y_n$$

The use of this formula requires that the known data points be equally spaced. For other variables in which the known data points were not equally spaced, straightforward linear interpolation was used to estimate missing values. These variables included, with the years for which values were estimated in parentheses, traffic citations and arrests (1948, 1959-1962) and all of the data taken from the Census of Manufacturing: wages of production workers, number of manufacturing establishments, number of wage workers in manufacturing, and the value added by manufacturing (1948-1953, 1955-1957, 1959-1962, 1964-1966, 1968-1971).

2. Insignificant variables were removed from equations one at a time beginning with the least significant.

3. Since the correlation matrix for this analysis is large, the matrix is not included here, but it can be obtained from the authors on request.

4. When attempting to enhance police strength, interest groups need not argue for more money to be allocated to the police. Wilson and Boland (1978) conjecture that police patrol strategies can be altered independently of expenditures on police to achieve greater arrest productivity. Arguing from a conflict perspective, Jacobs and Britt (1979) maintain that it may be less costly for police to enhance elite control over subordinate groups by giving the existing force a free hand.

5. The relatively weak negative coefficient for property crime at t-3 could be an artifact of collinearity between property $_{t-1}$ and property $_{t-3}$. Although the correlation between property $_{t-1}$ and property $_{t-3}$ is only moderate for time series data (r = .856), it would seem wise to test for problems with collinearity. First, standardized regression coefficients are not extraordinarily large (greater than |1|) when both t-1 and t-3 variables are in the equation. Second, the equation was reestimated with property $_{t-3}$ excluded and property $_{t-1}$ included. This specification leaves parameter

estimates relatively unchanged, with property $_{t-1}$ strong, positive, and significant. Similarly, when the equation is estimated with property $_{t-3}$ included and property $_{t-1}$ excluded, the t-3 coefficient remains weak, negative, and marginally significant. This stability in the equations suggests that collinearity is not a problem. Equations were also estimated excluding property $_{t-3}$ but including t-2, t-4, and t-5 specifications. None of these produces significant coefficients that eliminate autocorrelation.

REFERENCES

AMSDEN, A. H. (1981) "An international comparison of the rate of surplus value in manufacturing industry." Cambridge J. of Economics 5: 229-249.

APPLEBAUM, R. P. (1978) "Marx's theory of the falling rate of profit: towards a dialectical analysis of structural social change." Amer. Soc. Rev. 43: 67-80.

BARAN, P. A. and P. M. SWEEZY (1966) Monopoly Capital: An Essay on the American Economic and Social Order. New York: Monthly Review Press.

BLAUNER, R. (1970) Alienation and Freedom. Chicago: Univ. of Chicago Press.

BORDUA, D. J. and E. W. HAUREK (1970) "The police budget's lot: components of the increase in local police expenditures, 1902-1960," in H. Hahn (ed.) Police in Urban Society. Beverly Hills, CA: Sage.

CARO, R. A. (1974) The Power Broker: Robert Moses and the Fall of New York. New York: Knopf.

CHRIST, C. F. (1966) Econometric Models and Methods. New York: John Wiley.

DURBIN, J. (1970) "Testing for serial correlation in least squares regression when some of the variables are lagged dependent variables." Econometrica 38: 410-421.

GIDDENS, A. (1973) The Class Structure of the Advanced Societies. New York: Harper & Row.

JACOBS, D. (1979) "Inequality and police strength: conflict and theory and coercive control in metropolitan areas." Amer. Soc. Rev. 44: 913-925.

——— and D. BRITT (1979) "Inequality and police use of deadly force: an empirical assessment of a conflict hypothesis." Social Problems 26: 403-412.

KLEIN, L. R. (1968) "Theories of effective demand and employment," in D. Horowitz (ed.) Marx and Modern Economics. New York: Monthly Review Press.

KÜHNE, K. (1979) Economics and Marxism: The Renaissance of the Marxian System. New York: St. Martin's.

LAND, K. and M. FELSON (1976) "A general framework for building dynamic macro social indicator models: including an analysis of changes in crime rates and police expenditures." Amer. J. of Sociology 82: 565-604.

LANE, R. (1979) Violent Death in the City: Suicide, Accident, and Murder in 19th Century Philadelphia. Cambridge: Harvard Univ. Press.

LENSKI, G. (1966) Power and Privilege. New York: McGraw-Hill.

LOFTIN, C., R. C. KESSLER, and D. F. GREENBERG (1981) "Income inequality, crime, and crime control." Presented at the American Society of Criminology meetings in Washington, D.C.

MORISHIMA, M. (1973) Marx's Economics: A Dual Theory of Value and Growth. Cambridge: Cambridge Univ. Press.

MARX, K. (1968) "Introduction to the 'critique of political economy,'" in D. Horowitz (ed.) Marx and Modern Economics. New York: Monthly Review Press.

——— (1906) Capital: A Critique of Political Economy. New York: Random House.

McPHETERS, L. R. and W. B. STRONGE (1976) "Law enforcement expenditures and urban crime," in L. R. McPheters and W. B. Stronge (eds.) The Economics of Crime and Law Enforcement. Springfield, IL: Charles C Thomas.

OSTROM, C. W., Jr. (1978) Time Series Analysis: Regression Techniques. Beverly Hills, CA: Sage.

REISS, A. (1971) The Police and the Public. New Haven: Yale Univ. Press.

RUBENSTEIN, J. (1973) City Police. New York: Random House.

SHAW, C. R. and H. D. McKAY (1942) Juvenile Delinquency and Urban Areas. Chicago: Univ. of Chicago Press.

SHRYOCK, H. S. and J. S. SIEGAL (1975) The Methods and Materials of Demography. U.S. Bureau of the Census. Washington, DC: Government Printing Office.

SKOGAN, W. G. (1976) Chicago Since 1840: A Time Series Handbook. Urbana: Institute of Government and Public Affairs, University of Illinois.

SNYDER, D. and C. TILLY (1972) "Hardship and collective violence in France, 1830 to 1960." Amer. Soc. Rev. 37: 520-532.

TSURU, S. (1968) "Keynes v. Marx: the methodology of aggregates," in D. Horowitz (ed.) Marx and Modern Economics. New York: Monthly Review Press.

WEICHER, J. C. (1976) "The allocation of police protection by income class," in L. R. McPheters and W. B. Stronge (eds.) The Economics of Crime and Law Enforcement. Springfield, IL: Charles C Thomas.

WILDAVSKY, A. (1974) The Politics of the Budgetary Process. Boston: Little, Brown.

WILLIAMSON, J. G. and P. H. LINDERT (1981) American Inequality: A Macroeconomic History. New York: Academic.

WILSON, J. Q. and B. BOLAND (1978) "The effect of police on crime." Law and Society 12: 367-390.

ABOUT THE AUTHORS

RICHARD A. BERK is Professor of Sociology at the University of California, Santa Barbara. He has published widely in the fields of criminal justice and evaluation research. His most recent book in this field is *Money, Work and Crime: Experimental Evidence* (with P. H. Rossi and K. J. Lenihan, Academic Press, 1980). The issues discussed in his present chapter reflect an ongoing project with Sheldon Messinger on historical patterns of punishment in California, funded by the National Science Foundation.

WILLIAM F. EDDY is Associate Professor of Statistics at Carnegie-Mellon University. He is an associate editor of the *Journal of the American Statistical Association* and editor of *Computer Science and Statistics: Proceedings of the 13th Symposium on the Interface* (1981). His other research interests include statistical computing, data analysis, and the distribution of random sets.

JAMES M. ERVEN is a research assistant in the Center for the Study of Justice, Arizona State University. His research interests include the sociology of law and implementation phenomena.

STEPHEN E. FIENBERG is Professor of Statistics and Social Science and Head of the Department of Statistics at Carnegie-Mellon University. He is Chair of the Committee on National Statistics at the National Academy of Sciences and has co-edited a volume entitled *Indicators of Crime and Criminal Justice: Quantitative Studies.* He is also the author of several papers on the analysis of victimization data. Other research interests include statistical methodology, especially for the analysis of qualitative data.

DIANE L. GRIFFIN is a graduate research assistant in the Department of Statistics at Carnegie-Mellon University. She is completing her Ph.D. dissertation on the estimation of victimization rates using longitudinal survey data.

JOHN HAGAN is Professor of Sociology, Law and Criminology at the University of Toronto. His recent research is in the areas of crime, law, and criminal justice, and his articles have appeared in the *American Sociological Review,* the *American Journal of Sociology, Social Forces,* and the *University of Michigan Law Review.* Professor Hagan is on the editorial board of the *American Sociological Review* and a number of other American and Canadian journals.

MICHAEL HOUT is Associate Professor of Sociology at the University of Arizona. His current research is in the fields of stratification and demography. Other research focuses on comparing the occupations of husbands and wives in two-earner families. The present chapter reflects his interest in applying models developed for analysis of data on occupations to other kinds of data.

ALAN J. LIZOTTE is Assistant Professor of Sociology at Indiana University, Bloomington. His current research interests center on the policy implications for patterns of firearms ownership, discrimination in the legal process, and rape victimization. His research is almost always quantitative.

RICHARD McCLEARY is Associate Professor of Criminal Justice at the State University of New York, Albany. He is the author of several books and articles on time series analysis.

JAMES MERCY is currently affiliated with the Sociology Department at Emory University in Atlanta. He works with the Centers for Disease Control as an Epidemiologic Intelligence Officer assigned to the study of violence as a public health problem. An article with L. C. Steelman will appear in the *American Sociological Review* entitled "Familial Influence on the Intellectual Attainment of Children."

SHELDON L. MESSINGER, a sociologist, is Professor of Law at the University of California, Berkeley.

ERIC H. MONKKONEN is Professor of History at the University of California, Los Angeles. His most recent publication is "A Disorderly People? American Urban Order, 1860-1970," in the *Journal of American History* (December 1981).

BARBARA C. NIENSTEDT is a doctoral candidate in public administration at Arizona State University. She is currently employed as a research analyst for the Governor's Crime Commission and has worked as a time series consultant on several projects. Her research interests are methodology and applied statistics.

DAVID RAUMA is currently a Ph.D. candidate in the Department of Sociology, University of California, Santa Barbara. His interests include research methods and statistics, evaluation research, and criminology. His work has appeared in the *American Sociological Review,* the *Journal of Criminal Law and Criminology,* and *Social Science Research.*

MARJORIE S. ZATZ is Assistant Professor at the Center for the Study of Justice, Arizona State University, Tempe. She recently received her Ph.D. in sociology from Indiana University, Bloomington. Her current research interests include models of criminal justice processing and sanctioning, comparative criminology, and the effects of criminal justice processing on defendants' self-concepts.